The Gulf War

A Captivating Guide to the United States-Led Persian Gulf War against Iraq for Their Invasion and Annexation of Kuwait

Free Bonus from Captivating History (Available for a Limited time)

Hi History Lovers!

Now you have a chance to join our exclusive history list so you can get your first history ebook for free as well as discounts and a potential to get more history books for free! Simply visit the link below to join.

Captivatinghistory.com/ebook

Also, make sure to follow us on Facebook, Twitter and Youtube by searching for Captivating History.

Contents

Introduction

The late 1980s and early 1990s were times of significant changes. The Cold War was nearing its end as communism was slowly unraveling, new cyber and communication technologies were becoming more widespread, media was becoming more important and diverse, the economy was steadily growing in most parts of the world, and right-wing political parties and movements were gaining popularity across the globe. Amid all of those changes, a short but impactful war between the United States, aided by several allies, and Iraq occurred. Today it is known by many names, like the First Iraq War, Kuwait War, and, most commonly, the Gulf War or the First Gulf War. It was a rather short conflict, lasting just shy of seven months between late 1990 and early 1991. Yet it was still rather impactful as it showcased several essential innovations and changes in political and technological aspects of warfare, some of which are still part of modern conflicts.

The novelties brought by the Gulf War changed modern warfare in many aspects. It saw the rise of high-tech weapons, which were bolstered by the rising power of computers. No longer were the armaments assessed only by their pure destructive force; they were also judged on their precision and stealth. The sophistication of the US military might left the world in awe. The Gulf War also pioneered a new form of media coverage and control. It was probably the first live broadcasted conflict in history, with the daily video feed from the US bombers shown on cable networks. The combat looked so surreal for the ordinary observer that the audience quickly dubbed it the "Video Game War." These trends continue to this day, as the military industry works on new ways to incorporate the brain of a computer into a weapon. At the same time, the media, especially the internet, makes war and conflict a daily part of our lives.

Another important aspect of the Gulf War was that it was the first conflict after World War II that wasn't fueled by ideological confrontations between communists and capitalists, as the Soviet Union was on its last breath. It demonstrated that the Cold War had more or less ended by this point. Simultaneously, it shattered the beliefs of many who hoped that without the hostility of two blocs world would see fewer wars and conflicts. Thus, although small in size and limited in its immediate outcome and consequences, the Gulf War became a famous landmark in contemporary history. It signaled the break with the old ways of the 20th century and illuminated the path to our world today. For that reason, the Gulf War is still remembered and seen as an essential event in our recent past.

Chapter 1 – Iraqi-Kuwaiti Relations and the Prelude to the War

When talking about the Gulf War, it is not uncommon to start the story with the Iraqi invasion of Kuwait in mid-1990. It was, in fact, the immediate cause of the US-led allied intervention against Iraq. Nonetheless, to begin there would leave the narrative of this war somewhat two-dimensional, focusing solely on the combative aspects of the confrontation. To fully understand all the nuances, deeper causes, political undertones, and other elements of the Gulf War, it is essential to go further back in history. Only by stepping back can one get a better perspective and a fuller picture of the conflict.

Ottoman provinces in 1900, with Kuwait as part of Basra in the lower-right corner. Source: https://commons.wikimedia.org

The explanation of why and how the war started must begin with why Iraq decided to invade Kuwait in the first place. The question of Iraq-Kuwait relations can be traced back to the early 20th century to the end of World War I. Before that, both regions were an integral part of the Ottoman Empire. At the time, the city of Kuwait was a district of the Basra province, which was centered around the city of the same name in southern Iraq. However, Kuwait was only under the nominal rule of the Ottomans, as the Turks did not actually rule the city, and it led independent politics throughout most of the 19th century. And since the Ottoman Empire's power was disintegrating, the British tried to take control over the region. At first, they were interested in Kuwait as an important shipping port. In 1899, it became a British protectorate. That meant Kuwait was technically separated from Iraq; however, that bore little immediate consequences since both Kuwait and Iraq remained under the nominal control of the Ottomans. That changed during World War I, though, when the British forces moved into the Mesopotamian region, displacing the Ottoman rule with their own.

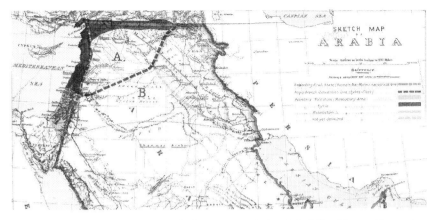

Map of the 1920 planned division of the Middle East (Iraq in yellow), without Kuwait. Source: https://commons.wikimedia.org

The factual control of the British was confirmed in 1920 by the League of Nations, the precursor of the modern-day United Nations. At first, Iraq was supposed to become an integral part of the British Empire. Yet after the Iraqi revolt that very same year, the British reconsidered that decision. In 1922, the Anglo-Iraqi Treaty was signed, and Iraq became a semi-independent British-administered kingdom. It was ruled by the Hashemite dynasty, which was an ally of the British. At the time, the British confirmed the separation of Iraq and Kuwait, honoring their promises to their local Kuwaiti allies. Nonetheless, many of the Iraqis felt that Kuwait should be a part of Iraq based on the fact that it was once a part of the Basra province. This idea persisted for a long time, forming the national goals of the Iraqi nationalists. Yet the Kuwaitis, with a brief exception in the 1930s, did not share their sentiment. In 1932, the British mandate ended. Thus, Iraq became an independent state. However, it kept its close ties with Britain both politically and, more importantly, economically. While Iraq was still under British rule, large oil fields were found, and the monopoly on exploration and production of oil in Iraq was given to the Iraq Petroleum Company. Despite its name, it was a British company. Nonetheless, it brought economic improvement to the Kingdom of Iraq. In contrast, Kuwait was going through a rough time, as its economy was left in ruins after World War I, and its status as a trading hub was fading.

Economic disparity, coupled with the fact that the Iraqi government was less oppressive, was enough for the citizens of Kuwait to attempt unification with Iraq in the late 1930s. However, their movement was unsuccessful as the British were opposed to it. Furthermore, the Iraqi government wasn't willing to give full-blown support because of their ties with Britain and because the local Kuwaiti government had imprisoned their leaders. So, the Kuwaitis mostly abandoned the idea of unification, though some remnants of it persisted until the 1950s. Nonetheless, Iraqi nationalists continued to view Kuwait as one of their territorial aspirations. Even so, for a short while, the international political situation stopped them from working on such plans. Still, the Iraqi government continued to negotiate with both Kuwait and Britain as they deemed the Iraq-Kuwait border to be improperly drawn by the British in previous years. These, combined with economic exploitation, pushed Iraq, especially its military circles, toward Nazi Germany. Thus, in 1941, a coup was staged, and a pro-Germany government was formed. Britain didn't wait too long. After a short war, Iraq was firmly under British occupation, and the pro-British government was reinstated. The British Army remained in Iraq until early 1948 when the Anglo-Iraqi Treaty of 1948 was concluded. Under it, Iraq was once again nominally independent but under substantial British control. A joint Anglo-Iraqi defense board oversaw the Iraqi military, while Britain continued to influence the foreign affairs of the Iraqi kingdom.

During the 1950s, the situation changed. By that period, Kuwait once again became quite wealthy, as it had become the largest oil exporter in the Persian Gulf. Oil was found in Kuwait as early as 1938, but it was not until the 1950s that the massive exploitation began, with several more oil fields being discovered during the decade. This meant that the Kuwaitis lost their economic incentive to become a part of Iraq. On the other hand, the Iraqi economy was still in crisis from World War II, as inflation was rising and the quality of life was falling. On top of that, the Iraqis, for most of the decade, were British pawns in the Cold War. Britain used them in an attempt to limit the penetration of communism in the Middle East. For some Iraqis, that was too much, as they felt that the interests of their people were being ignored. The idea of pan-Arabism was also spreading at the time, which was additionally fueled by the unification of Egypt and Syria into the United Arab Republic (UAR) in early 1958. Led by famed Egyptian President Gamal Abdel Nasser, the UAR aimed to unite all the Arabs into a single republic, free of Western interference and influence and under, to a certain degree, socialist economic ideas of equality. For the Kingdom of Iraq, that was a significant threat, and the British were also resentful of the new Arab state. Thus, Iraq and Jordan, both ruled by the same dynasty, united into a single state named the Arab Federation.

The newly formed state was supposed to counter the UAR's rising popularity; however, for at least some of the Iraqis, it was an unpopular move. They saw it as a way for the king and his political leaders to stay in power and maintain their entitled positions while the majority of the population continued to live in poverty. It was also seen as pandering to Western politics as it stood in the way of a united Arab people. In the end, this led to a military coup in mid-1958, where the monarchy was overthrown, and the Iraqi Republic was formed. The leader of the coup, Abd al-Karim Qasim, became the prime minister of the republic. His politics shifted Iraq closer toward the ideas of economic equality and pan-Arabism. Nonetheless, amidst these politics, Qasim still held on to the Iraqi nationalist notion that Kuwait should be a part of Iraq. His pressure on the southern Iraqi neighbor was highest in the summer of 1961 when Kuwait gained its independence from Britain. Qasim threatened with war and occupation, but he never fulfilled his threats. Most historians doubt he ever really planned to attack Kuwait, as it was defended first by the British then by the forces of the Arab League, a regional organization of the Arab states.

Pictures of Qasim (left) and Arif (right). Source: https://commons.wikimedia.org

Regardless, Qasim once again kept the Iraqi expansionist idea alive. He continued to use it in his politics until his fall in 1963 when another coup was staged, and he was executed. Colonel Abd ul-Salam Arif, a firm Iraqi nationalist, took his place, proclaiming a more friendly relation with Kuwait. However, it wasn't long before the Kuwaitis realized these were only empty words. The new regime indeed stopped threatening with an invasion, but it wasn't ready to recognize Kuwait as an independent state, and it also pressed hard on the matters of border disputes. Moreover, many members of the Iraqi government still thought that Kuwait should be a part of their country. The negotiations about recognition and borders were started that same year. Those dragged out for several years, with Kuwait even giving loans to Iraq, hoping to soften its position. In the end, these negotiations outlasted the Arif regime, as in 1968, another coup was staged in Iraq. This time, the members of the Arab Socialist Ba'ath Party took power. It was an Iraqi branch of the formerly unitary Ba'ath Party, whose main ideologies were pan-Arab nationalism and progressivism on a social basis. Once again, it seemed that a coup would bring the disputes between the two countries to a close.

Despite the auspicious readiness of Ba'ath Iraq to commence the negotiations, it wasn't long before they hit a dead end. As the new Iraqi regime was more distinctively socialist, with stronger ties to the Soviet Union, its relations with Iran quickly deteriorated. At the time, Iran was a monarchy; it had a shah as its head and was allied with the US and Britain. As such, it saw Ba'ath Iraq as a threat to its security, and the shah even tried to topple the new regime. However, this attempt was unsuccessful, and in 1969, it seemed that an Iranian-Iraqi war was imminent. The Iraqi government used this threat as a pretext to station its troops on parts of Kuwaiti territory. Even though Kuwait accepted this begrudgingly, its minister of defense stated that the Iraqi forces began deploying before an official agreement was made. The war between Iraq and Iran was avoided, but the Iraqi forces still remained in Kuwait, stating that until the Iraqi-Iranian border disputes were settled, the threat remained. In

1973, Iraqi troops tried to reinforce their garrisons in the territory of Kuwait, but the Kuwait Army tried to stop it. This event culminated with an exchange of fire in March of that year. This was enough for the Iraqi government to return to negotiations with Kuwait.

In the 1970s, the main territorial issue between Iraq and Kuwait was, in fact, over the islands of Warbah and Bubiyan. Those were located in the northwestern parts of the Persian Gulf and were quite close to both countries, though slightly closer to Kuwait. None of those islands had any riches on them, but their worth was strategic for both countries. For Iraq, they were essential to ease the control of the western parts of the Persian Gulf while protecting Umm Qasr, a vital Iraqi port near the Kuwait-Iraq border. On the other hand, for Kuwait, the islands were sort of a buffer zone, protecting it from being sucked into a war between Iraq and any other foreign force, mainly Iran. The islands were so close to the mainland, with Warbah being only 325 feet (100 meters) away from the Kuwaiti shore, that Kuwaiti sovereignty would be compromised if any foreign force were to hold it. Not to mention that any fighting there was bound to spill over onto Kuwaiti soil. On top of all that, these islands, though small in relative terms, represented a sizable chunk of Kuwait's entire territory. For this reason, the Kuwaiti government was unable to accept the Ba'ath regime's offers. Kuwait even rejected the Iraqi proposal of leasing the islands from them; in this offer, all other disputed lands would have been recognized as a part of Kuwait.

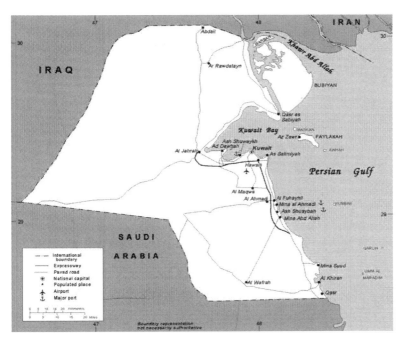

Map of Kuwait, including the contested islands. Source: https://commons.wikimedia.org

By 1975, the Iraqi government had to admit that, at the time, Iran no longer posed a threat to Iraq's security, and so, by 1977, it withdrew its forces from Kuwait. Kuwait continued to confirm its claim over the islands both politically, with a parliament resolution, as well as militarily, by building outposts on them. The status quo was to remain, even though the Iraqis still harbored territorial pretensions toward Kuwait. However, by the late 1970s, Iraq's focus was pointed at Iran. Both countries aimed at hegemony over the Persian Gulf, and despite an agreement signed in 1975, the territorial dispute burdened their relations. Nonetheless, it seemed that both sides were avoiding confrontation. This changed in 1979 with the Iranian Revolution. The monarchy was overthrown, and Iran became an Islamic republic under Ayatollah Ruhollah Khomeini. The revolution spurred a grand revival of both Persian nationalism and Shia Islam fundamentalism. As such, Iran not only retained its aspiration for becoming a hegemon of the Persian Gulf, but now, it also wanted to export its revolution to Iraq as well. Furthermore, in that very same year, Saddam Hussein, an Iraqi politician and general filled with nationalist ideas and dreams, enacted a purge in the Ba'ath Party and became the leader of both the party and the country. This only furthered distrust between the two now rather militant regimes, which led to both countries preparing for war.

Thus, in September of 1980, Iraq attacked Iran, using the Iranian Revolution as a pretext for war. In truth, the fears of Iraq were not unfounded. Shia Muslims were a relative majority in Iraq, and Khomeini saw that as a way to topple the Ba'ath Party from the inside, something he publicly said was his agenda. On the other hand, the Iraqi government wasn't satisfied with the 1975 agreement. It saw this as a chance to expand its territory since Iran was under sanctions and lacked international support. In the end, Iraq's ultimate goal was to become a regional superpower and the de facto leader of the Arab world. However, the Iraqi leaders underestimated the strength of Iran and its people. After some successes in late 1980 and early 1981, the Iraqi invasion was brought to a halt, and in 1982, Iran counterattacked. The war dragged on for years. Both sides had their successes and failures, accompanied by long periods of stagnation and trench warfare. By the mid-1980s, Iraq declared a policy of total war, with a widened military draft and ever-higher defense expenditures. Iran followed a similar path with the emergence of large volunteer armies, which often attacked in large human waves. Because of that, combined with the stalemate, this war reminded international experts of the trench warfare of World War I.

Iranian soldier in a trench during the Iran-Iraq War. Source: https://commons.wikimedia.org

During this conflict, which lasted much longer than the Iraqi leadership had expected, Iraq quickly ran out of resources. It had to take out loans to cover its financial losses. Its main financiers were its southern neighbors, Saudi Arabia and, more importantly, Kuwait. The Iraqi government asked them for money, representing itself as a defender of the Arab world against the Persian threat. Most of this was just Iraqi propaganda. However, the Iranians did bomb territories of Kuwait in the later stages of the war. Thus, there was a slight possibility that if Iraq was to fall, Kuwait would share its fate. For this reason, Kuwait was willing to lend as much money as Iraq asked for, and it became the main financial backer of its northern neighbor. The war dragged on until 1988. By this time, both sides were exhausted, and Iraq asked for peace, but Iran refused, mostly due to its fanaticism. Iraq then began threatening Iranian civilians with chemical warfare, pushing Iran to agree on a ceasefire in August of that year. The losses on both sides numbered in the hundreds of thousands, including tens of thousands of civilian victims. The war was settled on *status quo ante bellum*, meaning that despite claims from both sides and various observers, the conflict ended without a clear winner. Iraq didn't achieve its territorial expansion, while Iran failed to topple the Ba'ath regime.

President Saddam Hussein speaking by telephone at a frontline command to a field commander at East of Basra sector on Monday. The President personally directed the Iraqi battle against a fresh Iranian attack at the sector which started at midnight on Sunday. After crushing the Iranian attack and pushing the invaders back behind the border, the President returned to Baghdad

Iraqi propaganda during the Iran-Iraq War. Source: https://commons.wikimedia.org

Besides the massive losses in human lives, the most tangible result of the Iran-Iraq War was an economic disaster on both sides, with combined spending reaching to about 1.2 trillion dollars. Just prior to the war, Iraq had substantial financial reserves of about 35 billion dollars, with an annual income of about 26 billion dollars from oil exports. Its international debt was at a very low 2.5 billion. In fact, the Iraqi economy before the conflict with Iran was somewhat decent. However, the almost eight-year-long war devastated that relative prosperity. The oil production and exports were lowered, with Iraqi annual exports amounting to only about ten billion dollars. The reserves were spent, and the government accumulated a debt of about 130 billion dollars. The Ba'ath government was put under tremendous pressure as its population, which suffered rather high casualties, were becoming rather unsatisfied with the economic situation. The social upheaval was simmering beneath the surface. The position of the Iraqi government was further destabilized by the dissatisfaction of both the Shia and Kurdish minorities, which suffered significantly during the war. Furthermore, during the Iran-Iraq conflict, the Ba'ath government began shifting toward a more dictatorial regime under the strict rule of its leader, Saddam Hussein.

Faced with such a crisis, the Iraqi government began looking for a way to remedy its economic situation. It hoped to gather funds from revitalized oil exports. However, it ran into a problem that was out of its hands. The oil prices dropped due to the overproduction of certain countries, most notably Kuwait. Iraq turned to the Organization of the Petroleum Exporting Countries (OPEC), which, at that time, consisted mainly of nominally Iraqi-friendly Arab countries. Seeing that the cost of crude oil fell due to the overproduction, Iraq asked the member countries to limit their production and push the prices from about eight dollars per barrel to over twenty dollars. However, most of the OPEC members were reluctant to agree to this proposal as they were also experiencing their own internal problems. They sought to expand their production, not limit it, even though the Iraqi plan had a solid economic foundation. At the same time, the Ba'ath regime also sought financial help from its Arab friends. Iraq asked Saudi Arabia and Kuwait, as well as other Persian Gulf countries, for a moratorium on its wartime credits, as well as an immediate infusion of somewhere between thirty and forty billion dollars for reconstruction. The Iraqi propaganda tried to justify such demands by claiming that Iraq was fighting not only for itself but for all the Arabs, representing itself as a bulwark of the Arab world against the vile Iranians.

These demands, despite being accompanied by somewhat vague threats made by Saddam Hussein, were, of course, rejected by other Arabs. No one wanted to finance Iraqi wars, nor was anyone prepared to lower their oil production quotas. This left the Ba'ath regime in a dangerous position. It had to deal with the crisis or risk being toppled from within. Saddam and his government saw only one possible escape from this problem, which was to deal with Kuwait. It was, in fact, one of the countries that Iraq was most indebted to, and it was also a chief culprit of the oil overproduction. Furthermore, Kuwait had probably the weakest army in the Gulf region. On top of all that, the longstanding border dispute and pretensions of the Iraqi nationalists made it an even "sweeter" target for the Ba'ath government. Thus, by early 1990, Iraq started setting the stage for yet another invasion, one that was to be an even more enormous miscalculation than the war with Iran, causing an even wider economic crisis and more pronounced isolation.

Chapter 2 – Circumstances and Causes of the Gulf Conflict

The economic crisis and the nationalistic ideas were not the only reasons why Iraq decided to invade Kuwait, though they explain a substantial part of the Ba'ath regime's motivation. In the 20th century, no country, conflict, or alliance existed in an isolated bubble. On the contrary, every major event, every nation, and every war were tied together with the much larger, global picture. The Iraqi invasion of Kuwait and the Gulf War are no different, as they were not merely an isolated attack and a justified intervention.

The most crucial aspect of international politics after the end of World War II was undoubtedly the Cold War. Through it, the United States and the Union of Soviet Socialist Republics (USSR) competed for world dominance, usually through remote conflicts in third-world countries. The Middle East was also one of the regions where the influence and agendas of these two superpowers clashed. At the very beginning of the Cold War, the US had close relations with Israel, Iraq, Iran, Kuwait, and Saudi Arabia. These were maintained either directly or through the British, as they had held a strong presence in the region since the 19th century. On the other hand, the USSR began attracting revolutionary regimes of Egypt, Syria, Libya, and Yemen. Through the years, the political constellations changed a bit, with Egypt becoming more pro-Western in the 1970s, while Iraq became more pro-Soviet after the 1958 coup. The most significant change, however, was the position of Iran after 1979. Before the Iranian Revolution, Iran was probably the most important ally of the US in the region. The British even planned to make it the Western "policeman" of the region, tasked with maintaining security from possible pro-Soviet threats. Yet after the revolution, Iran became openly anti-American and anti-Western, which culminated with the Iranian hostage crisis that lasted from 1979 to 1981.

During that event, the US suffered substantial diplomatic humiliation, and US-Iran relations never recovered. Under Ayatollah Khomeini, Iran became one of the fiercest US adversaries in the world. That kind of political rift with one superpower of the Cold War would usually mean that Iran was turning toward the other superpower, the Soviet Union, something the USSR itself hoped for. The USSR was the first country to recognize the new regime of Iran officially, and it tried to create a more tangible relationship with the Islamic Republic of Iran. However, Khomeini saw communism as being in direct opposition to Islam, and so, those relations never expanded to anything concrete. As both superpowers were rebuffed, when the Iran-Iraq War began, both were leaning more toward Iraq. Yet, despite that, both Moscow and Washington continued to sporadically, and rather clandestinely, supply Iran with weapons during the war, most likely trying to win its allegiance in the grander scales of the Cold War. These attempts bore no fruit, however, leaving Iran somewhat isolated in its own aggressive stance toward the world. Yet both the Soviets and the Americans received worldwide backlash for those actions, especially from their Arab allies.

The signing of the Treaty of Friendship and Cooperation between Iraq and the USSR (1972). Source: https://commons.wikimedia.org

Due to this diplomatic failure with Iran, Iraq was left as one of the rare countries of the Cold War era that at one point was allied or at least cordial with both sides. On the one hand, since 1958, Iraq began turning toward the USSR, which began rapidly growing in 1968 and the start of the Ba'ath regime rule. Their close relations were at their peak during the 1970s, especially after 1972, which was when the Treaty of Friendship and Cooperation with the Soviet Union was signed. At the time, Iraq's diplomatic relations with the United States were almost nonexistent. The Ba'ath leadership was rather irritated by the US support of Israel, especially during the Six-Day War (1967) and the Yom Kippur War (1973), but also because they believed Americans were involved in the organization of an anti-Ba'ath coup in 1969, as well as the US somewhat covert helping the Kurdish rebellion in Iraq in the mid-1970s. These factors led the Ba'ath regime to believe that the US government was working on overthrowing them, which pushed them ever closer toward the Soviets. Yet more prominent leaders of the Ba'ath Party, like Saddam Hussein, were also eager not to become simple puppets of the USSR. Because of that, in the late 1970s, Iraq began turning toward other Western countries, mainly France, for armament.

Through these efforts, Iraq tried to lower its dependence on the Soviet Union, which was rather high at the time.

For the Iraqi-Soviet relations, 1979 was also an important year. The rise of Saddam Hussein in both the Ba'ath Party and the Republic of Iraq meant that the Ba'ath regime was even more inclined toward moving away from Soviet influence. Saddam didn't want to follow Soviet foreign affairs. He was keen on pursuing a more independent policy based on his own goals of making Iraq at least a local power, if not something more influential. Furthermore, the Soviet invasion of Afghanistan in that same year also put a significant strain on Iraqi-Soviet relations, as it was seen as a communist attack on a fellow Muslim country. After the Iran-Iraq War began, the Soviets attempted to gain diplomatic points by cutting off arms supplies to both Iraq and Iran in the fall of 1980, trying to force them to resolve their issues peacefully. However, the Ba'ath regime interpreted this as a further betrayal. This ban was quickly lifted, but the damage remained. Saddam and his regime began opening up toward the West even more, slowly establishing relations with the US. The United States was eager to form diplomatic ties with Iraq, both because it lost its influence over Iran but also because the Soviets would lose an ally.

As the Iran-Iraq War raged on, US-Iraqi relations began to improve. The United States started to send support, exporting technologies that had dual use in both military and civilian applications, and by 1984, official diplomatic relations were reestablished. By the end of the war, the relations between the US and Iraq were, at the very least, cordial, with the US officially siding with Iraq in an attempt to end the war. At the same time, the US intelligence services shared their intel about Iranian positions, helping the Iraqi generals plan their attacks. Yet despite that rather friendly stance toward the Americans, Saddam didn't cut off all relations with the Soviets. The USSR remained the primary source of armaments of the Iraqi Army, as well as one of their prominent foreign lenders, just behind Kuwait and Saudi Arabia. Thus, in the late 1980s, Iraq found itself to be in a

rare position of being in somewhat good graces of both compe'
superpowers. However, Saddam remained rather suspicious of both
the US and the USSR. It is known that despite being mostly pro-
Iraqi during the war, both superpowers did also sell arms to the
Iranians as well, even though only 23% of total weapons delivered
was sent to Iran. The Iraqi government remained under the
impression that both powers chose Iraq only because Iran refused to
cooperate.

On the other hand, both the US and the USSR realized that the
Ba'ath regime was a loose cannon, as it was hard to control and quite
volatile. Therefore, their support of the Iraqi government was never
fullhearted. Another problematic aspect of the Iraqi government was
that, through the years, it became outright dictatorial with a strong
leadership cult of Saddam Hussein, who was shown as the savior of
Iraq. The war only made it easier for him to transform Iraq into an
aggressive militaristic state. Saddam's grip over Iraq tightened, as he
was merciless toward any political threat that arose during the 1980s.
He showed even less sympathy toward the Kurds, an ethnic minority
in northeastern Iraq, who rebelled in 1983. Unsatisfied with the state
of things, combined with their long-lasting yearning for
independence, they rose up against the Ba'ath regime. Their revolt
was drowned in blood, as they were subjected to genocide through
the use of chemical warfare, which lasted until mid-1989. At the
same time, the Iraqi military also used chemical weapons against the
Iranians, against both military and civilian targets. Most of the
world, including both the US and the USSR, berated these actions.
The UN even issued several resolutions that condemned Iraq for
breaking the 1925 Geneva Protocol that banned the use of chemical
warfare. Nonetheless, neither superpower acted more tangibly, as
both had interests in an Iraqi victory, which would allow them to
maintain their influence in the region.

Despite the criticism for its actions and the use of chemical weapons,
Iraq remained on the good side of both the US and the USSR.
However, by that time, the Cold War was slowly coming to an end,

as the Soviet Union was going through its own economic crisis that was followed by political instability. This was followed by the fall of communist regimes across Eastern Europe, perhaps symbolized most vividly by the fall of the Berlin Wall in November 1989. Some historians even claim that with that event, the Cold War was officially over, as it became clear that the USSR had lost its ability to parry the United States. Thus, Saddam was eager to further his cooperation with the US, expressing his opinion in early 1990 that the Soviet Union was finished as a superpower. However, the position of the United States on this alliance was divided. The official Bush Sr. administration was eager to exploit the possibilities of working together with Iraq, as it hoped Iraq would become a pillar of stability and peace in the region, something that US diplomacy needed. On the other hand, public opinion, which could be most clearly seen in the media, was highly critical of Iraq and its regime, especially over the atrocities committed during the war.

Even the US Congress threatened Iraq with sanctions, although President George Bush Sr. spoke up against those kinds of actions. He also said he would use his powers of veto to stop any act of such type. Nonetheless, Saddam and his regime were both confused and annoyed with the dual stance the US held toward them. By mid-1990, he realized that Iraq was not going to receive full American support, especially since the main US ally in the region was Israel, a country with whom the Ba'ath regime had rather bad relations. Yet despite that, it seems that Saddam was confident that even though he wouldn't receive support, the US would not militarily oppose him. On the one hand, he calculated that the American government was too amicable for such work. On the other, he counted on his military prestige in the world, as he had one of the more massive and more experienced armies at the time. Saddam believed that the Vietnam War complex, the fear of high losses, in both lives and money, as well as the war in general, and the fear of prolonged conflict, would prevent the US from actively engaging him in the field of war. Concluding that his position in the worldwide political arena was strong enough, in early 1990, Saddam began planning his actions against Kuwait.

By early summer of that year, Iraq became more vocal against its southern neighbor, which was clearly noticed by the entire world. Some of the governments began fearing a new conflict would arise in the Gulf region. Most concerned was the Arab League, as this war would pose a threat to Arab unity and the entire region. The president of Egypt, Hosni Mubarak, directly intervened, managing to broker a meeting between Iraqi and Kuwaiti representatives in Saudi Arabia, in which he hoped to resolve their grievances peacefully. At the same time, Saddam called the US ambassador in Baghdad, April Glaspie, for a conversation. Together with his minister of foreign affairs, he expressed his dissatisfaction with the American stance toward Iraq, more precisely the critique of the US media, on July 25th, 1990. Glaspie tried to convince him that US President Bush Sr. wanted to better their relations based on the peace and prosperity of the Middle East. Saddam then turned toward Iraqi issues with Kuwait, claiming that low oil prices were devastating his country and that the price of 25 dollars per barrel was not high enough. He proceeded to claim that Kuwait's farms, installations, and border patrols were deployed and built as closely to the border as possible. Combined with the lowering of the oil prices, Saddam saw it as Kuwait placing excessive pressure on Iraq. Saddam then said that if the provocation continued, Iraq would respond to that pressure with force, as it seemed that course of action would be the only way to ensure his people would live decently.

He further added that some of the US citizens who were against Iraq went to Kuwait and other Gulf states to spread fear of his country and persuade them not to help Iraq rebuild. To these statements, Glaspie responded that the US had no opinion on Arab-Arab conflicts, like the one Iraq had with Kuwait. Today, some presume that the Iraqis interpreted this rather indifferent stance offered by the US ambassador as a sign that the US would not intervene in any possible future conflicts. Glaspie did show concern about the Iraqi forces building upon its southern borders, to which Saddam said he just wanted a fair solution to the issue. He further reassured her by saying that the Iraqis were not the aggressors, although they wouldn't accept aggression against them. For the US ambassador, that was enough to calm her, as she was informed about the pending meeting of the two sides in Saudi Arabia. Like most of the Arab League, she believed that the issues between Iraq and Kuwait would be settled there peacefully. Just several days later, on July 31st, the representatives of the two countries met in Jidda (Jeddah) under the patronage of Saudi Arabia, which wanted to act as an "Arab older brother" and ensure peace between them.

The exact details of the direct talks in Jidda are unknown. However, through the later accounts of some of the actors, there is a general idea of what was discussed. Iraqi representatives voiced what their government saw as Kuwaiti transgressions. There was the matter of border disputes, most notably in the case of the Rumaila oil field. The bulk of that oil field lies within Iraqi territory, but its southern tip was in Kuwait. Iraq claimed that its entirety should be de jure Iraqi, while it was de facto partially under Kuwaiti soil. Thus, from the Iraqi perspective, the Kuwaitis were guilty of border transgression and stealing their oil and revenue. Furthermore, Iraqis accused the Kuwaitis of lowering oil prices through overproduction, as well as denying their request for Iraq to fly commercial flights through Kuwaiti airspace. It is also reasonable to assume that the issues of Iraqi debt and the matter of Warbah and Bubiyan were brought up, as they were also an essential part of the Iraqi-Kuwaiti dispute. It seems that the Kuwaiti representatives rebuffed all the accusations and demands of their counterparts without presenting any constructive proposals since the Iraqis left on August 1st. Later, the Kuwaitis claimed that the Kuwaiti side offered to forgive Iraq's debt, or at least part of it, and allow the Iraqi military to construct some facilities on the contested islands. The issue of the Rumaila oil field was offered to be settled through an arbitration of some sort.

It is possible that these offers were only hinted at but not recognized by the Iraqis. It is also not impossible that the Kuwaitis only stated this later to present themselves in a better light in the dispute. Of course, it is not out of the question that by that time, the Iraqis had abandoned the idea of resolving this disagreement through peaceful diplomacy. Regardless, the end result of the Jidda conference was the opposite of what everyone had hoped for. The Iraqi government was left even more unsatisfied and irritated, while the tensions between the two neighboring countries worsened. On August 1st, Saddam held a state meeting where the Iraqi leadership discussed how to proceed. From their point of view, Kuwait had, once again, exhibited no desire to find a compromise while the state of the Iraqi economy and their regime was in dire straits. By that period, several smaller revolts against Saddam's oppression erupted, as the people were feeling the ever-growing pressure of the economic crisis. The Ba'ath leadership either had to act now or see itself fall from power. The only solution for them was a military invasion. Saddam's decision to turn once again to an act of open aggression was eased by his belief that the US would not intervene directly and that the Soviets were too weak to do anything. On top of that, he thought that the Arab League would be more sympathetic toward his position, even hoping that the Arab League would bolster his position as a pan-Arab leader.

Thus, on August 2nd, 1990, Saddam ordered an attack on Kuwait. With that, the Gulf War began. It was a result of a combination of the longstanding Iraqi border issues with Kuwait, the ideology of Iraqi nationalism, the internal economic and political crises of the Ba'ath regime, and the international political atmosphere of the ending of the Cold War, as both superpowers showed little resolution in dealing with the issues of the Persian Gulf region.

Chapter 3 – The Invasion of Kuwait and the Beginning of the War

As the talks between Kuwait and Iraq were slowly falling apart in July 1990, Saddam and his high command met to discuss further steps. It became evident for them that the only way to gain what they wanted was the use of military force. It was something they thought they could get away with due to the international political stage of that time. But the question still remained on how far they should go.

It seems that, at first, the Iraqi leadership wanted to use their military to occupy only the disputed islands of Warbah and Bubiyan, as well as the South Rumaila oil field. But on August 1st, 1990, Saddam Hussein gathered the Revolutionary Command Council (RCC), where he proposed to annex all of Kuwait instead. He opted for that option for two main reasons. One was geopolitical, as Kuwait was seen as a longstanding puppet of Western superpowers whose leaders counted on their support for defense. Thus, Saddam concluded that Kuwaiti rulers would rely on a war of diplomatic attrition in case of partial occupation. In that scenario, the US would eventually put pressure on him to withdraw, leading to his political fall from power in Iraq. In addition to that, Saddam calculated that if the Iraqi Army was to hold all of Kuwait, foreign forces had less chance to intervene militarily. Saddam counted on the fact that by having power over the whole coast of Kuwait and Iraq, Iraq's enemies would have a hard time landing and pushing them back, as he believed that the Saudis would allow foreign troops on their land. Mixed with that was the second reason, the ideological one. He needed a boost of popularity at home, and Kuwait was traditionally seen as a part of Iraq by the nationalists. Saddam hoped this move would help him stabilize his position while at the same time enhancing his image as a true pan-Arab leader.

At this point, it would be easy to simply blame only Saddam Hussein for the beginning of the Gulf War. Yet, even though his advisors may have been surprised, they weren't unsupportive. Both the military and the political leadership were enthusiastic about Saddam's new approach toward the problem of Kuwait. His generals assured him of Iraq's military capabilities, while his advisors told him the Americans were not ready for another war. With the full support of the higher leadership of Iraq, on August 1st, 1990, Saddam ordered his troops to attack. On August 2nd at 1:00 a.m. local time, Iraqi forces invaded Kuwait. Over 100,000 Iraqi soldiers, supported with about 2,000 tanks, poured over the border to the disbelief of almost the entire world. Despite the fact that Iraqi troops had been piling up on the frontier throughout July, many observers saw this move as pure aggressive posturing to force the Kuwaitis to comply. No one thought that after the exhausting war with Iran that Saddam would so eagerly enter a new conflict, least against a fellow Arab country with whom he was actively negotiating to resolve their issues. Not even Kuwait was ready, as its army wasn't fully mobilized and prepared. Thus, within just twelve hours, the Iraqi forces had swiftly overrun the 16,000 strong Kuwait Army, seizing the entire territory of its southern neighbor. The Gulf War had officially begun.

A meeting between Mikhail Gorbachev and George Bush Sr., where they signed an agreement to end the use of chemical weapons (1990). Source: https://commons.wikimedia.org

It wasn't long before it became apparent that Saddam had made a mistake in his calculations. In a matter of days, most of the world condemned the invasion of Kuwait, demanding the withdrawal of Iraqi troops. It wasn't surprising that most of the Western allies of Kuwait, like the United States and the United Kingdom, were spearheading this kind of diplomatic pressure, both in the media and in the United Nations. What was surprising to some, if not all, was that the Soviet Union, which had a habit of opposing US actions in the UN, backed American diplomacy. The Soviet president at the time, Mikhail Gorbachev, was willing to support the United States on this matter for several reasons. For one, at the time, the Soviets themselves were going through an economic crisis, and Gorbachev sought to ease it by opening up to the West and counting on their aid. If he was to oppose them, that financial aid would stop. And for that same reason, the Soviet leadership was, at the very least, annoyed that Saddam, their ally on paper, chose to act on his own accord. His actions were damaging both to the Soviet Union's reputation and to their much-needed yet improving relations with the

West. Thus, the USSR was ready to issue a joint statement with the US that condemned the Iraqi invasion. In fact, this readiness for the cooperation of the Soviet Union proved to be an important factor in how the Gulf War was to proceed.

Apart from Soviet support, the Arab League also played an essential role in future events. Most of the members, apart from Iraq and Libya, were opposed to Saddam's actions, seeing it as unnecessary Arab on Arab violence. On the 3rd of August, the League passed a resolution calling for the withdrawal of Iraqi troops and to resume peaceful negotiations while at the same time objecting to a possibility of a non-Arab force intervention. This left Saddam without a single considerable ally by the second day of the Iraqi occupation of Kuwait. Yet Saddam's position wasn't ultimately doomed; however, American diplomacy was only gearing up. In the following days, US diplomats were busy on two fronts. One was international, working in the UN for another resolution following the first one issued on August 3rd, which just condemned Iraq's actions. The Americans knew that simply scolding the Iraqi government wouldn't do much to persuade Saddam to retreat. Thus, they began working on a resolution that would enact total economic sanctions on Iraq. For that, the US once again had to attain the Soviet Union's compliance, as its power of veto in the UN Security Council could stop any future resolutions from being passed.

Luckily for the Americans, the economic blockade was acceptable to the Soviets as a peaceful solution. Besides the USSR, it was also crucial that the immediate Iraqi neighbors accepted these sanctions as well. Most of them were ready to comply. The only possible issue was Turkey. Though opposed to the Iraqi invasion, Turkey was worried that those sanctions could damage its economy. This potential problem was resolved by the US sending financial aid to Turkey, with the caveat of questioning Turkey's future in NATO (the North Atlantic Treaty Organization) if it refused to comply. Thus, the diplomacy of the United States secured these economic sanctions, which were first imposed by UN Resolution 661 on

August 6th and then enacted by Iraq's neighbors. The economic pressure on Iraq was furthered by the fact that the US and most of the other countries also froze any Iraqi or Kuwaiti assets abroad. However, the American leadership felt that this alone wasn't enough, so simultaneously, it was working on securing its positions if military actions were to become necessary. For that, the US diplomacy team worked firstly with the Saudis and the rest of the Arab League. Their first issue was to secure the permission of Saudi Arabia for the deployment of foreign troops on their territories, which was vital for bypassing Saddam's coastal defenses.

Traditionally, the Saudis were against any non-domestic forces being allowed on their soil, especially non-Muslim ones. Thus, at first, Saudi Arabia, together with other members of the Arab League, tried to mitigate a peaceful solution. It seemed that Saddam was open toward the possibility of an Arab meeting that would resolve the issue. Still, Egypt, which was a longstanding adversary of Iraq, issued a statement condemning Iraq's invasion. After that, Saddam lost his trust in the Arab League. Nonetheless, the Saudi king was still hoping a peaceful solution was possible. At that time, US intelligence showed the Saudi leadership that Iraqi forces were massing on their borders, warning them that they could be next. It is unlikely that Saddam was planning to continue his push into Saudi Arabia as well, but this was enough for the Saudis to be concerned. On top of that, if Kuwait were to remain under Iraqi control, it would become the largest producer of oil in the OPEC countries, dethroning Saudi Arabia from its leadership position in that organization. After much debate among the highest officials of the country, Saudi Arabia decided to allow the deployment of American troops in their territory. They circumvented the traditions by officially inviting them on their soil on August 6th, 1990. By the next day, the first US troops were deployed in Saudi territory. This invitation was also sent to other Arab countries. Egypt and Morocco answered the call rather quickly.

US Defense Secretary Dick Cheney and Saudi Minister of Defense Sultan al-Khair (late 1990). Source: https://commons.wikimedia.org

By then, Saddam saw that he and his advisors had made a colossal miscalculation. Military intervention by land was now possible. Furthermore, the United States was the first to deploy troops, showing an apparent willingness on their part to enter into a potential armed conflict, while the majority of the Arabs, as well as the Soviet Union, were supportive of the American efforts against Iraq. However, this wasn't enough to make Saddam fall back. Instead, the Iraqi government stubbornly retaliated by first proclaiming Kuwait to be a republic with a provisional government on August 7th and then pronouncing the full annexation of Kuwait on the very next day. It was to become the nineteenth province of Iraq. In that period, Iraqi forces tightened their grip over Kuwait by arresting and executing possible leaders of the opposition. At the same time, the systematic looting of Kuwait was in progress. Iraqis took various everyday and luxurious goods, industrial and electronic equipment, and much more, topping it off with about two billion dollars found in Kuwait's central bank. This helped alleviate the immediate effects of the economic sanctions placed on Iraq. On the foreign diplomacy front, Saddam tried to gain some credibility by attaching Palestine to the invasion of Kuwait. He stated that Iraq was prepared to withdraw from Kuwait if Israel would retreat from the Palestinian lands. Once again, he was presenting himself as a grand pan-Arab leader, fighting not only for the needs of Iraq but for a broader Arab cause as well.

Meeting between Saddam Hussein and the prime minister of the brief Kuwaiti puppet regime (1990). Source: https://commons.wikimedia.org

This attempt was fruitless. Most of the Arab countries continued to view Iraq as an aggressor and a possible threat, while the US had no intention of acknowledging any connection between the two issues. That, of course, wasn't surprising, as Israel was probably the closest ally the United States had in the Middle East. Thus, the Kuwaiti issue entered into a stalemate. The allied forces were still steadily massing on the Saudi-Iraqi border, while Iraq stubbornly refused to withdraw from Kuwait. From a superficial first glance, Saddam's refusal to end his occupation could be seen as either his hubris and his belief that Iraq could fight against the world or as his nationalistic dictatorial appetite. However, those are, at best, only partially true. Saddam wasn't delusional, and he didn't believe that his armies could attain a straight-up victory against the international forces piling up on Iraqi borders. However, he believed they could bog down their advances in a military stalemate, inflicting high enough casualties to force them to negotiate with him. Also, Saddam's expansionistic appetites weren't as high as most have represented. It seems he would have been satisfied with gaining only the Warbah and Bubiyan Islands and the rights to the South Rumaila oil field. Most likely, he was using the annexation of Kuwait as a bargaining chip.

The problem was that, for most of the world, especially the US, there was nothing to negotiate about. Iraq had to withdraw unconditionally. However, Saddam couldn't accept that. Due to the rising economic crisis caused by the sanctions, which led to rationing and rising dissatisfaction among the common Iraqis, his position was shaky—and not only his but that of the entire Ba'ath leadership. Thus, a withdrawal without any gains would most likely mean their fall from power and possibly something even harsher. The Iraqi government at that time couldn't afford another meaningless war that brought nothing except an economic crisis. The United States was deaf to these facts, but other countries were aware of it. For example, French President François Mitterrand attempted to find a peaceful solution by asking for the withdrawal of all foreign troops in Middle Eastern territories, including Iraqi soldiers in Kuwait, international forces in Saudi Arabia, and Israeli soldiers stationed in the disputed territories. Furthermore, he advocated for allowing the Palestinians to have their own country, as well as the reduction in armaments of the entire region, from Iran to Morocco. Of course, this grandiose plan was rejected by pretty much everyone. Despite that, during the stalemate of the issue, several other nations tried to mediate peace in the region, both for the sake of peace itself but also to gain international prestige of solving such a major problem. In hand with that was the fact that the non-oil-producing countries were also economically suffering from rising oil prices.

Most notable was the Soviet attempt, as Gorbachev wanted to avoid any possible use of international forces against Iraq. In early

October, the USSR sent its representative to Baghdad to attempt to persuade the Iraqis to stand down. Gorbachev even sent a letter directly to Saddam through that mission. Yet the Soviets were unable to promise any gains for Iraq. Thus, once again, Saddam had little choice but to continue his occupation, as the US was not prepared to give in the slightest to Iraq's demands. In fact, since the Iraqi invasion, it seemed that the United States was approaching this issue with the policy of "no negotiation"—either Iraq would withdraw or the US would use any force necessary. However, it seemed that the United States was set on going through the United Nations to preserve its international credibility. That choice could be linked with the experience of the Vietnam War, in which much of the world saw the American engagement as unjust. For that reason, the US used the UN Security Council to exert pressure on Iraq. With UN Resolution 660, which was passed on August 2nd and condemned the Iraqi invasion, US diplomacy relied on UN resolutions for legitimacy.

The US Navy ship stationed in the Persian Gulf, enforcing the economic blockade (late 1990/early 1991). Source: https://commons.wikimedia.org

For example, after UN Resolution 661 was enacted, which was a mere three days after the Iraqi aggression started, most of the world agreed to enact economic sanctions on Iraq. Nonetheless, some countries were either unwilling or incapable of respecting that embargo. For that reason, UN Resolution 665 was adopted on August 25th, 1990, which allowed a naval blockade to impose the economic restrictions on Iraq. This gave the US and its chief ally Great Britain permission to use force if needed to enact the sanctions, something that has been seen as a violation of international law by some. Another issue that arose, which was processed by the UN, was of the foreign nationals (those who were not Iraqis or Kuwaitis) who were left in Kuwait after the occupation. There was a concern about their treatment by the Iraqis, who, through rations, focused their supplies to the military. Seen as hostages since the Iraqi authorities didn't permit them to leave after the occupation, the UN passed Resolution 666 on September 12th, which demanded that the Iraqi government provide them with the necessary supplies. Some countries, like Cuba and Yemen, saw the root of this problem in the economic blockade, which caused famine in Iraq and forced the Ba'ath government to ration their supplies. Yet the UN continued to pass resolutions that became increasingly aggressive in their tone. For example, UN Resolution 674 from late October stated that "the Council will need to take further measures" if Iraq didn't comply with the demands.

The main reason for that was the fact that the US and the British began more actively voicing their opinion that the use of military force was going to be necessary. Thus, the governments of those countries began to gather support for such a move while they tried to persuade other nations that the economic sanctions had failed and that the use of force was the last resort. There have been many critics both at the time and even today who think that there wasn't enough time for the blockade to work and that, given enough time, Saddam would have withdrawn peacefully. However, the governments of both the United States and Great Britain were worried that time was working in favor of the Iraqis. Their main concern was that differences among the permanent members of the UN Security Council would arise, making it rather difficult, if not impossible, for it to adopt any further resolutions about the Iraqi invasion. This fear was fueled by both Soviet and French actions, as those two permanent members of the council were the loudest proponents of a peaceful solution to the Kuwaiti crisis. Thus, by late November, the UN Security Council met and voted on what was to become known as UN Resolution 678. In it, the UN gave a de facto ultimatum to Iraq, stating that the Iraqi forces had until January 15th, 1991, to withdraw from Kuwait. If the Iraqi government failed to comply, the UN granted the Coalition states the right to use "all necessary means" to liberate Kuwait.

The resolution itself was highly criticized, both morally and legally. The main issue that many had against it was the fact that the United States had used somewhat unethical means of persuasion while lobbying for it. For example, the Soviets were quite literally bought off with about seven billion dollars in aid from several countries, including some that were pressured by the US, among them Saudi Arabia, which provided one billion alone. Apart from that, the US itself promised considerable food shipments to the Soviets. On the other hand, the Chinese, who were traditionally against any foreign interventions, were won over by diplomatic favors. The US was to lift economic sanctions imposed after the Tiananmen Square incident in 1989, and a Chinese minister of foreign affairs was to be received by the White House. In return for those favors, China would abstain from voting on the resolution. Other uncertain members of the UN Security Council were also convinced by either economic or diplomatic incentives. This was enough to leave only two countries in the council against it, Cuba and Yemen, which refused to be bribed or intimidated. Yemen, one of the poorest countries at the time, suffered for its "no" in the UN. The US, the International Monetary Fund, and the World Bank immediately stopped their aid program to Yemen, which was worth about seventy million dollars, while Saudi Arabia expelled about 800,000 Yemeni workers.

However, this "stick and carrot" policy used by the United States to secure the votes in the UN Security Council wasn't the only reason why some have questioned the morality of UN Resolution 678. In the eyes of some observers, the very act of awarding the right to use force to the US-led Coalition was, in fact, contrary to the UN's founding charter. Through this action, the UN was avoiding direct responsibility and accountability for the use of this military force, allowing for the unilateral control and orchestration of world policy by the United States. Furthermore, by doing so, the UN encouraged a departure from the predominantly peaceful and humanitarian values and purpose it was founded on. On the other hand, some jurists have deemed this resolution to be invalid. In their interpretation, the Chinese decision to abstain from voting made the decision void, as the UN Charter states that the decisions of the Security Council need to have concurring votes of at least nine out of fifteen members, including all five of the permanent members. Nonetheless, for the majority of people at the time, including the members of the council, this wasn't an issue. The Chinese themselves were persuaded not to vote against such action. Still, their foreign policy didn't allow them to vote for military intervention in a sovereign state.

In the end, the issues of morality and legality of UN Resolution 678 was of little concern for the Coalition forces, primarily the United States. Those who questioned it were in the minority. Most of the world accepted it since their actions had been officially approved by the United Nations, as it gave the forces the legitimacy it needed for their involvement in a conflict with Iraq. The table had been set for a full-blown war between the Coalition forces and Saddam's army, as most analysts realized that there was little chance for the Iraqis to actually retreat. From November 29th, 1990, to January 15th, 1991, the world was simply waiting for the clash of the two forces to begin.

Chapter 4 – Military Forces of the Gulf War

To fully understand the events of the Gulf War, its course, and its resolution, we first must delve into the states of the opposing forces. On one side was the Iraqi military machine, which had recent combat experience. On the opposing side stood a collation force led by the US military. It had much to prove, both because it still held the cross of the Vietnam War but also because it was the leading power of the emerging post-Cold War world.

On paper, the Iraqi Army was a formidable foe. It had around one million active soldiers, though the estimates vary, with a possibility of doubling that number through the full conscription of men from 18 to 34 years old. Divided into about 60 divisions, it was also supplied with somewhere between 5,500 and 6,000 tanks and about 8,000 armored personnel carriers (APC). It had air support of around 200 helicopters and 900 airplanes, combined with a formidable air defense network that consisted of approximately 10,000 anti-aircraft artillery (AAA). The Iraqi Navy was the only part of Saddam's war machine that seemed unimpressive, which is not surprising due to Iraq's rather short coastline. However, the strength of the Iraqi Army was daunting only when looking at these raw numbers on paper. If one delves deeper into details, it quickly becomes evident that the military power of the Iraqi Army was largely blown out of proportion by the media coverage of the time. Several central issues plagued the Ba'ath forces. Firstly, even though its army was large in number, not all of them were stationed in the south. Some stayed near the Syrian and Iranian borders in case of a surprise attack. On top of that, the majority of the Iraqi soldiers were conscripts that lacked morale and combat training.

Despite how Western media represented them, not all of the operational Iraqi soldiers of that time were active combatants in the Iran-Iraq War. There were substantial numbers of fresh young recruits as well. Even worse for the Iraqi high command was the low morale. The Ba'ath regime was struggling with popularity at the time. This meant that at least some of its soldiers were disillusioned with their leadership, wondering if the new war would bring any better fortunes than the last had. In contrast to those ordinary foot soldiers stood a truly experienced high command, which was, in fact, highly adept at coordinating mass movements, artillery attacks, and complex maneuvers. Their specialty was the strategy of static defense, backed by mobile reserve, which was used against the Iranians. However, the problem that arose was that the Iraqi headquarters had trouble with the common units executing those orders. The notable exception was the Republican Guard, which consisted of better-trained and better-equipped soldiers who were rather loyal to Saddam's regime. In fact, during the Gulf War, it seems that the Republican Guard was the only part of the Iraqi Army that actually exhibited high capability in maneuvering and cooperation. Yet its numbers were rather low (about 150,000), and for most of the conflict, they were used as strategic reserves.

Another issue that plagued the Iraqi Army was how varied its arms and equipment were. In the decade leading to the Gulf War, Iraq was gathering weapons from where it could. As mentioned above, those came from the Soviet Union and their allies, such as France, China, Brazil, etc. That kind of diversity in equipment was a logistic nightmare for the Iraqi high command. It had to concentrate similar types of vehicles and weapon systems into the same units to facilitate both their usage and maintenance. Furthermore, as Iraq faced a substantial economic crisis, most of the arms were not kept in great condition, while the army, in general, lacked the spare parts needed to repair them. The industries in Iraq were producing some of the extra parts needed, though often not in the quantities needed. Yet more delicate products like microelectronics were above their technological capabilities. In some rare cases, the Iraqi military industry was even able to produce arms improvements based both on indigenous and foreign designs. Nonetheless, the lack of spare parts plagued most of Iraq's armed forces. It was not uncommon for Iraqi engineers to practice "mechanical cannibalization" when the need for them was too dire. This problem also meant that their equipment was often underperforming, further lowering the battle effectiveness of the Ba'ath forces.

Abandoned Iraqi T54/55 main battle tank. Source:
https://commons.wikimedia.org

However, probably the most crucial problem of the Iraqi Army was the fact that most of the units were equipped with outdated arms. For example, on paper, roughly 6,000 tanks seem like more than a formidable force. Yet, in reality, more than half of those tanks were Soviet T-54/55 tanks or their variations from China (T-59/69-I) and Romania (TR-77), which were originally designed and first produced in the years following World War II. This means that more than half of the Iraqi armored forces were equipped with tanks that were based on 45-year-old technology. The second most used tank in the Iraqi Army, totaling roughly at 1,200 vehicles, was the Soviet T-62. Although it was a feared model when it was first introduced in 1961, the T-62 was a thirty-year-old design by the early 1990s, making it outdated as well. Most of the modern tanks the Iraqis had were the Soviet T-72s, which came in several variations. There were roughly 500 of them in service, and they were mostly attached to the Republican Guard units. These T-72 tanks were sometimes modernized with some modifications, but the basic design was developed by the Soviets in 1971, twenty years prior to the Gulf War. Besides those Soviet-based tanks, the Iraqi Army also had some other tanks, most notably 200 to 300 British Mk. 3/3P and 5/5P Chieftains, which were captured from the Iranians. However, these were also designed and produced in the 1970s, which was when they were sent to the Iranians, who were, at the time, still British allies.

The Iraqi Army had similarly outdated models of the APCs, with most being variations of the Soviet BTR-50 and BTR-60, which were first designed in the 50s and 60s. Unlike the tanks, the types of APCs used by the Iraqis varied more. They used the French AMX 10P and Panhard M3, Italian OTO Melara Type 6614, Brazilian ENGESA EE-9, Yugoslav M60-P, Chinese YW531, and many more. However, most of these were also designed in the 1960s and early 1970s. Probably the only exception was the Soviet BMP-2, which was designed in 1980, but those were attached only to the Republican Guard. Iraqi artillery was similarly varied, mostly consisting of the Yugoslav variation of the 122mm Soviet D-30 howitzer, which was based on a design from the 60s, and the Soviet 100mm D-44 and 130mm M-46 from the 1950s. Along with them, the Iraqi Army used the Austrian GH N-45, South African G5, and the US M114 155mm howitzers. Besides the common types of artillery, Saddam's forces also used self-propelled artillery (SPG) and multiple rocket launchers (MRL), which each made up about 10% of the Iraqi artillery. The Soviet 2S1 and 2S3 SPGs were the most common, but Iraq's military also had the French Mk F3 and GCT, as well as the US M109A1s, which were captured from Iran during the war. The Soviet models were from the 1970s, while the French and the US ones were designed during the 1960s. The MRLs used by the Iraqis were mainly Soviet BM-21s from the 1960s and Brazilian Avibras Astros II from 1983.

In contrast to that, the Iraqi Air Force was much less varied. The bulk of its power consisted of Soviet MiG-21, MiG-23, Mig-25, and MiG-29. They also used Soviet Su-7, Su-20, Su-22, Su-24, and Su-25. The most modern of these fighter jets were designed during the late 1970s, and they weren't as numerous in the Iraqi arsenal. Along with them, they used French Mirage F1 fighter-bombers from the 1960s and Soviet Tu-16 and Tu-22 bombers from the 50s and 60s. Much more feared among the Coalition forces were the NATO-designated Scud tactical ballistic missiles, most of which originated from the USSR. The most used of these was the so-called Scud-B, originally named by the Soviets as R-17, which were from the late 1960s. The Iraqi military industry also developed its own Al Hussein (al-Husayn) in the late 1980s. These were basically upgrades of the Soviet R-17 to increase their range. Both of these weapons were capable of carrying not only conventional but also chemical, biological, and even nuclear warheads. Their range, which went up to 400 miles (644 kilometers), meant that, on paper, the Iraqi Army could possibly even bomb the Coalition's support units and headquarters. However, neither the tactical missiles nor the conventional artillery ended up posing any real threat to the Coalition forces.

Two Iraqi-modified Al Hussein *missiles displayed with their launchers at the 1989 Baghdad arms exhibition. Source: https://commons.wikimedia.org*

When talking about handheld weaponry, Iraq's military used various types of Soviet AKM and AK-74 assault rifles, which were modifications and modernizations of the famous AK-47. Besides those, the Iraqi Army used the Soviet-made RPD and RPK light machine guns, as well as medium and heavy SGM and PK machine guns. The Iraqis also employed Soviet SPD and Yugoslav M-76 sniper rifles. The most commonly used pistols were the Soviet T-33 and the Iraqi *Tariq*, a design that was based on the Italian Beretta M1951. Another commonly used weapon was the famous RPG-7, an anti-tank handheld rocket launcher. All of these handheld arms were designed during the 60s and 70s but were still rather useful on the battlefield. All in all, when looking at the Iraqi Army, it wasn't a force to be taken lightly, as it had its strengths. However, when looking back on how the world and the news saw Saddam's forces, it becomes clear that most of the media exaggerated its powers to a high degree. At the same time, the Coalition generals were rightfully preparing for the worst possible scenario, which only helped with the overplaying of the Iraqi force. All of this stemmed from the Vietnam experiences of the US Army, which was, at the time, still fresh, both in military circles as well as in the media.

For that reason, the US military was tackling this conflict with the utmost seriousness. The sheer number of American soldiers deployed showcases this. There were roughly 697,000 US soldiers in the Gulf War, which constituted almost three-quarters of the total Coalition forces, which numbered around 955,000 men. In comparison, at the peak of US involvement in the Vietnam War in 1969, there were 543,000 American soldiers deployed. Another essential difference between the US Army during the Vietnam War and the Gulf War was its morale and training. After the failure of the Vietnam War, the US government abandoned the draft system, making the United States military a volunteer-based, professionally trained force. Despite that, some of the media at the time represented the US Army as unprepared for desert warfare, similar to how it was unprepared for the jungles of Vietnam. However, the American forces were regularly training for the harsh conditions of the Middle East in the Mojave Desert, which is located on the border of California and Nevada, as well as in parts of Texas and New Mexico. Some of the troops were even training in Egypt during the 1980s in the form of military exercises with the Egyptian military. Thus, the US soldiers were both well-prepared and high in morale and fighting spirits.

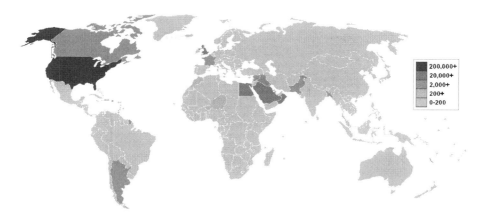

Countries that were members of the Coalition and their approximate contribution in personnel. Source: https://commons.wikimedia.org

Besides the US, 34 other countries contributed to the Coalition forces. Among the more numerous were the Saudi forces, with somewhere between 60,000 and 100,000 men, and the British, with about 53,000. Egypt sent 20,000 men, while France deployed 18,000 personnel. Other notable contributors, whose number of soldiers were above 2,000, were Morocco, Syria, Kuwait (those forces that managed to elude the Iraqis during the invasion), Oman, Pakistan, Canada, the United Arab Emirates (UAE), Qatar, and Bangladesh. Others sent a rather insignificant number of men, no more than a few hundred. It is important to note that most of the soldiers from the countries with smaller contributions were actually support staff, like engineers, medics, and base guards, while others participated only in aerial warfare. So not all of the countries were engaged in direct combat. Looking at the raw numbers of the men who were deployed, one thing becomes clear. The Coalition forces were not outnumbered, as some media actually portrayed them. The two sides of this conflict were quite equal in size. It is even debatable that the Iraqis were somewhat outnumbered, as some estimates state only about 650,000- to 750,000 Iraqi soldiers were deployed in the theater of war. Others were stationed in northern regions, though it was possible for them to join the fight if needed.

Egyptian soldiers in the Coalition in prayer. Source: https://commons.wikimedia.org

But the raw numbers and overall training of the US Army, backed with the rest of the Coalition forces, were not the only advantages they held over the Iraqis. The United States military deployed about 2,000 M1A1 Abrams battle tanks, which were 1986 upgraded versions of the 1980s M1 Abrams. These tanks were the most modern and technologically advanced of the time. The M1A1 had a range of fire above 8,200 feet (2,500 meters), while most Iraqi tanks topped at 6,600 feet (2,000 meters). It also had better optics, higher precision, and higher penetration, as well as better armor. Not even the Soviet T-72 was a match to it; it was only comparable to the couple hundreds of M60A1/A3 Patton and M551A1 Sheridan tanks that were used as a backup for the M1A1. Those were older US tanks that were designed and modified during the late 1960s and early 1970s. The United States ground forces were also equipped with about 3,000 APC, most being M2 and M3 Bradleys, which were designed in 1981. Those were equipped not only with a 25mm cannon but also with a TOW missile launcher, making it capable of engaging tanks as well. Besides those, amphibious assault and reconnaissance vehicles, like the LAV-25, which was designed in 1983, and the older AAVP-7A1s from the 1970s, were used. Also present was the M113A2, which was a 1970s modification of the 1960s design.

M1 Abrams tanks in the Iraqi Desert with an M2/M3 Bradley APC in the back. Source: https://commons.wikimedia.org

All in all, the US Army fielded both more advanced and better-equipped ground vehicles than their Iraqi counterparts, which were, of course, also better maintained. Besides the United States, their partners in the Coalition forces also brought their own vehicles. The British brought the FV4030/4 Challenger 1 tank, which, like the Abrams, was a modern tank that entered service in 1983. Besides that, they had the FV 4003 Centurion Mk 5 AVRE 165, a modification from the 1960s. Their APC arsenal had both older vehicles, like the FV432 Trojan that was initially designed in the 1960s, and more modern ones, like the FV 510 Warrior, which entered service in 1988. The French brought their AMX-30B2 tanks, which were modernized versions from 1979 of the original AMX-30 design. Like the British, they brought both older APCs, like the Panhard AML-90, which were used by the Iraqis as well, and the newer AMX-10 RC that was designed in the 1980s. The Saudi Arabian Army brought over 500 tanks, including the French AMX-30S and the US M60A3, which were both older designs from the 60s and 70s. They also had about 1,500 APCs, which were likewise a mixture of older US and French designs, like the M113A1 and the

Panhard AML-60/90. The Kuwaiti forces in exile were armed with the British FV4201 Chieftain from the 1960s, as well as with the M84-AB, a Yugoslav 1984 modernization of the T-72, which made them more comparable to the Abrams and Challenger tanks. As for the APCs, the Kuwaiti forces used both the Soviet-made BMP-2 and the US M113A1.

The Egyptians, although they had the Soviet-made vehicles in their arsenal, sent only units equipped by the US M60A3 and M113A2/A3. On the other hand, Syria, a longstanding ally of the Soviets, deployed mostly T-54 and T-62 tanks, along with a few of the T-72 models. Along with them, they used BMP-1 and BTR-60 APCs, which meant they used rather identical vehicles as the Iraqi Army did. In fact, seeing how varied the Iraqi equipment was in general, the Coalition forces were quite wary of possible friendly fire, which proved to be more dangerous than the Iraqi resistance. All in all, when comparing the vehicle firepower of the Iraqi Army and the Coalition forces, it is rather apparent that the latter had the upper hand. Most of their armored transport and tanks were more modern and technologically advanced, while manpower was, at best, minimally better on the Iraqi side, if not equal. This kind of superiority extended even further when it came to aerial warfare. There, the Coalition forces had not only the advantage in technology and modernity but also in numbers. With over 2,000 aircraft, they had more than double the entire Iraqi Air Force.

Most of these planes were the US F-14, F-15, F-16, and F/A-18, which were all designed and built during the 1970s. Alongside them were the French Mirage F1 and Mirage 2000, with the latter being developed in the late 1970s and introduced into service in 1984, as well as the British/French SEPECAT Jaguar and British/German/Italian Tornado, which were both from the 1970s. These were fielded by various members of the Coalition forces, like the French, the British, the Saudis, the Kuwaitis, and the Italians. The US forces also brought some of their older planes, like the B-52 and F-4, but it also employed more unconventional aircraft like the

EF-111A Raven, which was introduced in 1983 and used for electronic warfare. More famous than the Raven was the F-117A Nighthawk, a stealth bomber also introduced in 1983 that used advanced technology to remain undetected by enemy radar systems. The Coalition air efficiency was furthered by the use of the Airborne Warning and Control System (AWACS), which were airborne radar systems in the form of the Boeing E-3 Sentry as well as the Boeing KC-135 Stratotanker, a military aerial refueling aircraft, which allowed for attacks deeper into Iraqi territory. Apart from the combat planes, the Coalition forces also used various transport aircraft, like the C-5B Galaxy and the C-130 Hercules.

A US F-117A Nighthawk stealth airplane. Source: https://commons.wikimedia.org

The aerial superiority of the Coalition forces was furthered by several hundred various helicopters, most of which were deployed by the US military. They ranged from the quite modern attacking helicopters, like the H-64 Apache, which was introduced in the 1980s and armed with the most advanced technologies at the time, to the bit older Vietnam-era AH-1 Cobra. Besides them, an even wider array of transport helicopters was used. The US forces fielded some of the older types, like the iconic HU-1 "Huey," as well as the CH-47 Chinook and the OH-58 Kiowa, all three from the Vietnam War period. But the American forces also used more modern ones, like the UH-60 Black Hawk, which was introduced in 1979, and the highly modified version of that helicopter, the MH-60G/HH-60G Pave Hawk, which entered the service in 1982. Some of the common types used by other members of the Coalition forces were the French SA-342 Gazelle and SA-330 Puma, designed in the late 1960s and early 1970s, and the British WG-13 Lynx, which was introduced in 1978. Thus, when the allied airpower is summarized, it becomes clear that the Iraqis were severely overpowered. Yet, thanks to their air force and anti-aircraft defenses, they could at least try to confront the Coalition forces. That kind of uneven balance of military might was even more apparent when it came to naval warfare.

On the one hand, the Coalition forces brought all kinds of ships, ranging from the impressive aircraft carriers and battleships to mid-size destroyers, frigates, and missile cruisers. The classes of these ships were mostly designed in the 1960s and 1970s, but this meant little, as the Iraqi Navy had only a limited number of small missile boats and common patrol vessels, ships that posed virtually no threat to the Coalition naval forces. What is a more important aspect of the Coalition marine power was its ability to strike with Tomahawk long-range subsonic cruise missiles. It was more than a worthy answer to the threat of the Iraqi Scuds. Introduced in 1983, these missiles used the most advanced technology of that time, combining high precision and high destructive power, as well as carrying 1,000 pounds (450 kilograms) of conventional warheads. As such, they proved to be a valuable addition to the Coalition artillery power. In this field, the main superiority of the Coalition forces once again laid in the fact that their weapons were a generation ahead of the Iraqi Army. The most commonly used SPGs were the US M109A2/A3 and M110A2, which were modernized versions of the original design, as well as the French AMX-30 AuF1, which was introduced into service in 1977. Besides those, there was a wide array of howitzers used, like the US M198 and the French Tr-F1, which were both introduced in 1979 and had 155mm guns, as well as some older models and smaller calibers. The artillery firepower was topped with the most modern MLRs, the US M270 from 1983.

A US ship firing a Tomahawk missile during the Gulf War. Source: https://commons.wikimedia.org

The handheld weaponry of the Coalition forces also varied a lot, but the most important ones were the US M16A2 assault rifle, an upgraded and modernized version of the Vietnam War M16. It was made more reliable and precise, entering into wide service in the mid-1980s. Alongside them were the British SA80 L85 from 1985 and the French FAMAS from 1979, as well as some Soviet AKM and AK74 that were used by Egyptian and Syrian soldiers. These were accompanied by numerous types of pistols, snipers, shotguns, submachine guns, and other assault rifles. The Coalition soldiers also used anti-tank weapons, like the older M72 LAW, and, at the time, the most modern US-built AT-4, as well as the British LAW 80, with the latter two both being introduced in 1987. The Egyptians also brought the Soviet RPG-7. In the end, it is also important to note that the superiority of the Coalition forces wasn't only based on weapons but also on other technological innovations, like, for example, the

GPS (the Global Positioning System). These innovations, though some were in their infancy like the GPS, provided easer communication, maneuvering, navigation, and cooperation of separate units. That kind of advantage in the logistics capabilities department isn't something to look over, as they largely enhanced the effectiveness and precision of all actions and missions performed by the Coalition forces, even though most of the technology was only available to the US Army.

After comparing the two sides of the Gulf War, one thing becomes clear. This wasn't close to a fair fight as the media sometimes reported it. The Iraqi power was largely blown out of proportion, making it look like a mini superpower, which it wasn't. On the other hand, when talking about the Coalition forces, the focus usually remained on several of their most grabbing pieces of equipment, like the F-117 and Tomahawk missiles, which, though important, weren't the whole story. Behind those stood a massive force armed with the most modern weapons. Iraq stood basically no chance against the allies, even though many thought otherwise.

Chapter 5 – The War among the Clouds

While the diplomats and politicians negotiated and talked, trying to find a peaceful solution to the Iraqi-Kuwaiti problem, the generals were planning their future battles as January 15th, 1991, was closing in. The Iraqis were preparing their ground defenses, hoping that they would be able to cause enough casualties to the Americans to force them to the negotiating table. However, the US generals had other plans. Their first goal was not on the ground but high above, among the clouds.

The Coalition forces, under the overall command of US General Herbert Norman Schwarzkopf Jr., were focused on avoiding the possibility of the Gulf War becoming the "new Vietnam." Thus, instead of merely pushing the entire ground forces toward the Iraqi defenses, the US command opted to soften the target by aerial attacks first. The plan was to use the 2,000 fighting aircraft amassed by the Coalition forces to first establish total air superiority and then proceed with strategic bombings of the Iraqi positions. Of course, the tactic of aerial dominance wasn't something new. It was actually something that the US military had used since World War II. It was even applied during the Vietnam War. The difference was that by the early 1990s, the technology was advanced enough for bombings to be precise enough to transfer the dominance of the air to dominance on the ground. During the Vietnam War, despite the massive bombings, the effects were somewhat limited due to the inability to precisely pick out desired targets. However, in the Gulf War, the Coalition air force was using guided bombs, allowing for almost surgical precision. This meant that a fighter-bomber armed with only two so-called "smart bombs" could achieve the same result as roughly 100 B-17 bombers during the Vietnam War.

Despite that, the US-led Coalition command wasn't about to rely solely on technology. The United States generals devised a plan named "Instant Thunder," conveying a stark contrast to the "Rolling Thunder" from the Vietnam War. Unlike its predecessor, Instant Thunder was to be a short and decisive offensive air campaign, based on careful planning and coordination. The territory in the Kuwaiti theater of operation was divided into 33 square boxes, 30 miles (48 kilometers) in diameter, allowing for the precise allocation of specific areas to a specific group of airplanes. With those "killing boxes," the aerial command, which was located in the Saudi capital of Riyadh, was capable of forming air tasking orders (ATO), a schedule that matched the Coalition assets to their specific targets, all within a coherent timetable. Thus, every aspect of the air operations was tightly managed, from the take-off to the bombing run to the return back to base. With that, the Coalition forces, or, to be more precise, the US forces, as more than 1,800 aircraft were operated by the Americans alone, were ushering in a new aerial strategy by combining cutting-edge technology and careful planning, creating a blueprint that was to be used in all future US-led campaigns.

In contrast to the modern and aggressive approach of the US, the Iraqi Air Force relied on a somewhat outdated, defensive, and quite passive approach. Two factors could explain this tactic. The first was that during the Iran-Iraq War, the Iraqi Air Force suffered substantial losses while carrying out its strategic bombing raids. That shaped the

Iraqi aerial tactics toward a more defensive stance. Thus, their planes never left Iraqi airspace or went on attacking missions against the Coalition forces. This strategic complacency was only furthered by the fact that most of the Iraqi airplanes were outdated, even though the Iraqi Air Force had some of the slightly newer MiG-29 fighters. At the same time, they were outnumbered, at least, by three to one. The second factor that contributed toward this defensive and passive stance was Saddam's reliance on his air defenses. Armed with thousands of AAA guns and surface-to-air (SAM) missiles, which were guided by a formidable radar detection system, the Iraqi air defense was supposed to be a much more viable threat to the Coalition air force than the Iraqi Air Force itself. Furthermore, Iraq was also dotted with rather resilient bunkers and shelters made from reinforced concrete, which were key for weathering the Coalition bombings. The key idea behind Iraq's strategy was to endure the aerial attacks until the Iraqi Army could inflict enormous casualties upon the invading ground forces.

An abandoned Iraqi MiG-21 and MiG-25 in the background (after the Gulf War). Source: https://commons.wikimedia.org

Some military experts argued after the war that Saddam would have been in a far better position if he had sent his planes to attack the Coalition forces while they were building up, utilizing the Iraqi Air

Force before it lost its aerial superiority. From a purely military point of view, this would have possibly been a better solution. However, the Gulf War was more than just a combat situation. For the entire period between August and January 15th, there was a potential peaceful solution to the Gulf crisis. And despite how the media portrayed Saddam, he wasn't totally disillusioned or craving for war. Thus, during that entire period, the Iraqi Army stayed on its side of the border, with only one incident of a single Iraqi aircraft entering Saudi airspace and leaving before the incident could escalate into something more. Saddam and his high Ba'ath officials were aware that if they pulled the first punch, they would lose all international credibility and possibility to achieve anything through negotiations. Yet, at the same time, they weren't ready to back down and withdraw from the occupation of Kuwait without gaining something tangible. Thus, when January 15th came, the Iraqi troops were still holding their positions. With the passing of the deadline, the Coalition forces were prepared and fully authorized by the UN to act.

The first Coalition attack came on January 17th, around 3 a.m. local time, transforming the original defensive operation, which was codenamed "Desert Shield," into an offensive campaign known as "Desert Storm." The first attack was made under cover of night by eight AH-64 Apache helicopters, which were, in turn, guided by three MH-53 Pave Low helicopters. They flew low, fast, and without lights, attacking two Iraqi early warning radar systems near the Saudi-Iraqi border. Those radars were quickly destroyed with precise firepower, creating a radar-blank corridor through the first lines of the Iraqi air defenses. The helicopter squadron, known as Task Force Normandy, was fired upon but managed to get back to base without any losses. The mission was a success, allowing further attacks by the Coalition airplanes. However, the attack itself was quickly reported to the Iraqi command, alarming it to the upcoming attack. In a matter of minutes after the initial strike, the first of 700 Coalition planes flew toward Iraq. The primary targets of the preliminary air raids were strategic positions connected with Iraqi aerial defenses, like radar stations, airfields, the Nukhayb air defense center, and other government installations. Most of the targets were in southern Iraq, but on the first night, F-117A Nighthawks, as well as Tomahawk missiles fired from US Navy ships, also hit Baghdad.

During the first 24 hours, the Coalition air force flew just shy of 3,000 sorties. Among them was also one of the longest bombing raids in history, as seven B-52Gs flew from a base in Louisiana, located on the mainland of the US, and crossed half the globe to reach Iraq. There, they launched cruise missiles and returned home, covering 14,000 miles (22,500 kilometers) in about 25 hours. Other B-52 bombers were sent from the Indian Ocean, carrying large conventional bombs that killed both with their blast and a concussion shockwave, as their explosions made the ground tremble like in a manmade earthquake. This made those bombing missions reminiscent of the Vietnam War raids, where the US employed similar tactics. The Iraqi Air Force remained mostly inactive, just as Saddam planned, with only a handful of direct confrontations with the attacking aircraft. Those usually ended with the Iraqi planes losing the duels. Thus, the Coalition forces quickly took over the control of the airspace, as the Iraqi air defenses proved to be an inadequate match to the technologically advanced Coalition aircraft. By January 23rd, the US Air Force proclaimed that general air superiority was achieved, though it seemed more like total dominance. In those first six days, over 12,000 sorties were flown, with the US generals claiming only 5 out of 66 Iraqi airfields as still being functional, while an estimated 95 percent of the Iraqi defensive radar system was destroyed. On the other hand, the Coalition losses were minimal to almost nonexistent.

Iraqi MiG-25 destroyed in an aircraft bunker by a US laser-guided bomb. Source: https://commons.wikimedia.org

The inactivity of the Iraqi forces when it came to aerial defense took most of the Coalition generals by surprise. They expected a much fiercer opposition by the supposedly fourth strongest army in the world. Yet the Iraqi airplanes were mostly kept on the ground. The only notable exception was an attempted attack on the Saudi Ras Tanura oil production facility. On January 24th, the Iraqi Air Force sent two F1 Mirages, accompanied by two MiG-23s on the only offensive aerial mission during the war. It ended up as a failure, as the two MiGs abandoned the F1 fighter-bombers upon seeing two Saudi F-15s, which proceeded to shoot down the lone Mirages. However, the Iraqis never planned to get involved in a more serious aerial confrontation, a decision that could be dually assessed. From one perspective, it was a huge mistake, as it left the airspace undisputedly in the tight grip of the Coalition forces. This air superiority proved to be an important factor in the later Coalition attacks. At the same time, it could be seen as a conservative decision to save the Iraqi air flotilla. The Iraqi commanders were aware of its inadequacy to stand up to their enemies, which had advantages both in numbers and technology. The Iraqi high command turned to the Scud missiles instead.

By opting to use only ballistic missiles for the offensive actions, the Iraqi Army was capable of targeting rather distant objectives without sacrificing any lives. On top of that, the Scuds had a chance of damaging the Coalition troops' morale, similar to the German World War II V1 and V2 rockets. Yet, like their German predecessors, the Scud missiles were not known for their precision and effectiveness. Nonetheless, after the first Iraqi ballistic weapons were fired on January 18th, the so-called "Scud hunting missions" became one of the top priorities of the Coalition air force. Many feared that Saddam would order the use of chemical or biological warheads, and so, they designated the Scuds as one of their primary targets. However, during the entire Gulf War, none of the 88 ballistic missiles fired by the Iraqis was armed with anything else except conventional warheads. Despite that, the Scud attacks proved to be problematic to the Coalition forces, or, to be more precise, to the US, which led the joint military action. Nearly half of those missiles were fired toward Israel, an officially neutral country that wasn't a part of the Coalition. It was yet another attempt to bind Israel to the Iraqi issue.

Israeli civilian building hit by an Iraqi Scud (January 1991). Source: https://commons.wikimedia.org

Saddam Hussein hoped to provoke Israel into retaliating by bombarding cities like Tel Aviv and Haifa. Such action would have almost certainly broken up the allies, as the Arab states would have backed out of the Coalition, which would then lose its international integrity and Saudi territory as its base. In the worst-case scenario for the US, the conflict could turn into another Arab-Israeli War. To prevent that, the Americans installed Patriot SAM systems that were modified to intercept the Iraqi Scuds, offering protection to the Israelis. Despite that, the Patriot system wasn't full-proof, and many of the Iraqi missiles had their warheads intact even after being struck by Patriot projectiles. The Scuds would miss their targets but would still explode and cause damage. Thus, the US, as well as their European allies, offered more than 1.1 billion dollars as compensation for the damages and casualties caused by the Scuds. Their only condition was for Israel to not fire back at Iraq. That stipulation was followed by the Israelis. By the end of the war, 42 missiles had struck their territory, killing roughly 70 civilians and injuring about 250 more, while several thousand houses and buildings were damaged.

The rest of the Iraqi Scuds were fired at Saudi targets, both civilian and military. However, Saudi Arabia suffered lower civilian casualties, most likely because its cities were smaller and less dense. Only one Saudi civilian lost his life, while 78 others were injured. Military losses were much higher, as one Scud missile, which was actually hit by the Patriot defense system, managed to hit the US barracks in eastern Saudi Arabia. It killed 28 soldiers and injured over 100 more. That made it one of the most effective attacks of the Iraqi Army over the entire course of the war, at least in terms of casualties and damages caused. Because of all that, by the second week of the aerial operations, about one-third of the Coalition sorties were aimed at destroying Scud missile launchers. It was an effort that mostly proved ineffective, as it was hard to locate them in the vast Iraqi deserts. At the same time, the allied forces believed they had exhausted their original highly strategic targets, like airfields, radars, and weapons depots. Thus, their missions began shifting toward hitting the Iraqi ground forces, their communications, and their resources. Among them were also so-called "dual-use" targets, such as public highways, bridges, railways, etc.

From a military point of view, those were all valid targets, as they provided Iraqi troops with much-needed supplies and communication lines. However, since those were also used by civilians or were in the vicinity of civilian structures, their bombardment was also threatening the noncombatant population. Of course, civilian casualties were something that public opinion did not tolerate, and the Coalition forces quickly came under pressure from spectators. US President Bush Sr. tried to calm the backlash by claiming that the US Army was doing everything in its powers to avoid and minimize civilian casualties. He further blamed his opponents for relocating Iraqi military and strategic installations, like command and communication centers, into civilian neighborhoods. Those accusations weren't unfounded, as Saddam realized that noncombatant losses could improve his diplomatic position. Because of that, on January 25th, he recalled Western journalists to Baghdad, allowing them to witness firsthand the results of the supposed Coalition precision bombings. Most of them were shocked to realize that despite what the US high command was declaring in press conferences, the accuracy of their attacks was less than ideal. First of all, only about 10% of the total bombs dropped by the Coalition forces were so-called smart bombs. The vast majority were conventional bombs with limited precision, leaving sufficient room for errors.

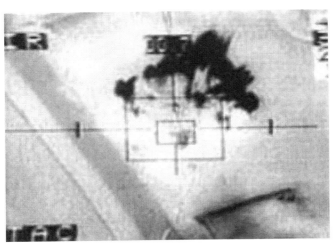

A still image from a video feed of a laser-guided smart bomb.
Source: https://commons.wikimedia.org

Yet this was far less surprising for the journalists than the fact that even the precision-guided missiles were less than perfect. For example, in the city of Diwaniya, a telecommunications tower approximately 150 feet (45 meters) tall was entirely missed by four different air raids, but surrounding hotels and market shops were hit and severely damaged or destroyed. They further saw that private houses, schools, and even hospitals were accidentally hit, causing dozens of unnecessary civilian casualties. The issue wasn't always the matter of precision of the laser-guided bombs, as sometimes faulty intel gathered by Coalition surveillance marked the noncombatant public structures as viable targets. An example of that was the bombing of a civilian shelter in the suburbs of Baghdad. It was inaccurately distinguished as an Iraqi command center and was subsequently attacked. The result was somewhere between 500 and 1,000 civilian deaths. Among the victims were about 100 innocent kids. To worsen the situation for the Coalition forces, the estimation of the effects of the aerial raids in the first two weeks of the bombardments proved to be exaggerated. Reevaluation of the original reports showed that about two-thirds of the Iraqi airfields were still at least somewhat operational, while Iraqi defenses had regained about 20% of its radar capabilities. This was most likely caused by the fact that the Coalition bombings only damaged some of the Iraqi equipment, knocking it out only temporarily.

Apart from that, the Iraqi Army managed to preserve most of its tanks, anti-aircraft artillery, and Scud launchers, as well as mobile communication systems. Also, due to the lack of active air defense, the Iraqi Air Force lost less than half of its fighting force. Most of their planes were destroyed on the ground, but over 100 of them flew over to Iran, where they surprisingly found sanctuary. On top of all that, the Iraqi aerial defense began shooting down Coalition aircraft, though not in any significant numbers. Iraq started showing signs of putting up a slightly stiffer resistance. Because of that, the allied air force proved to be less efficient than expected. At the same time, the Scud attacks intensified, causing even more trouble for the Coalition command, as it had to keep resources allocated to finding and destroying Iraqi ballistic missiles, which further lowered the effectiveness of the bombing campaign. For that reason, the US generals leading Operation Desert Storm were forced to prolong the aerial bombing campaign for much longer than what was initially expected, slowing down the four-stage-plan of the attack on Iraq. After two weeks of air raids, the Coalition was still fulfilling the first two stages. The first one was the bombing of strategic command and communication targets, and the other one was attacking strategic reserves and disrupting communications between the Iraqi leadership in Baghdad and the troops stationed in Kuwait.

What was even more troubling for the United States was the fact that the almost universal support to the Coalition mission was slowly winding down beginning in late January. The Soviet Union began expressing concerns that the bombing tactics employed would lead to the destruction of all Iraqi infrastructure, crippling the country for an extended period. Gorbachev himself was also worried that the Gulf War could expand and cause even wider conflicts. Other nations began expressing their disagreement with the direction the Coalition was heading, as well as the conduct of the war, especially concerning civilian casualties. Among them were even the members of the Coalition itself. The French minister of defense claimed that its ultimate goal was not only to expel Iraqi troops from Kuwait but also to overthrow the Ba'ath regime. Because of his disagreements with France's involvement in the war, he even resigned from his office in late January. Coming to a similar conclusion, Egyptian President Mubarak and Saudi King Fahd bin Abdulaziz declared their troops would not fight on Iraqi soil, limiting their actions only to Kuwaiti territory. Even worse, a Pakistani general who was appointed to the Coalition task force accused the West, mainly the US, that the entire war was a conspiracy to weaken the Muslim world by destroying Iraqi power.

Similar sentiments were rising among the ordinary population as well. The anti-war protest began spreading across the world. The most massive ones were held in Muslim countries more sympathetic to the Iraqi cause, like Algeria, Morocco, and Sudan, where the number of protesters went as high as 300,000 to 400,000. On a much lesser scale, protests and strikes also spread among the US allies and Coalition members, including France, Italy, Spain, Turkey, and Germany. Anti-war rallies spread as far as Australia and Japan. Some of these protests were violent, with burning fires in front of the United States embassies and blocking the American military bases. Anti-war rallies appeared in the US as well, most notably in Washington DC, though they represented only a clear minority of the American public. The support of the war there was undeniably still high. However, this made President Bush Sr. and his administration aware that a prolonged war wasn't an option. The US would quickly lose the support of the world, turning the American soldiers into villains once again. Thus, the Coalition pressed on with the bombings, beginning phase three of the plan, which was pressuring Iraqi troops on a tactical level. It was the preparation for the final stage of the war, a ground invasion into both Kuwait and Iraq.

Anti-war protest in New Orleans (US) in January 1991. Source: https://commons.wikimedia.org

As the bombs continued to fall on Iraq, the Ba'ath regime began to reconsider the benefits of the war. It was becoming clear to Saddam and his high officials that the Gulf War would bring more destruction than anticipated. At the same time, the idea of the "mother of all battles," as Saddam called it, turned out to be wishful thinking. The possibility that the Iraqi troops would fight off the inevitable ground invasion was slim to none, while the aerial bombing began taking its toll. The Coalition losses were minimal, while the Scud attacks proved to be more of a nuisance than a viable threat. Luckily for the Ba'ath regime, even though the Soviets weren't their allies in this war, they were still looking to protect their influence over the country. Thus, in early February, Soviet and Turkish officials called for an end to the devastation of Iraq in a joint statement. At the same time, the Iraqi diplomats started showing interest in negotiations and peace. This prompted President Gorbachev to send an envoy to Baghdad on February 12th to persuade the Ba'ath government that a diplomatic resolution was possible if it accepted requirements set by the UN resolutions. The Soviets hoped to avoid a land war, which would not only be costly in the number of lives lost—it could also mean the fall of the current Iraqi regime.

The crumbling Soviet Union, like many other nations, suspected that the end goal of the US-led Coalition was to topple the Ba'ath regime, replacing it with a more pro-Western government. It seemed that the Soviets managed to convince the Iraqi leadership of that during their contacts in early February. As a result, Saddam's regime declared on February 15th that it was open to finding a peaceful resolution of the conflict. However, the US was only accepting an immediate and unconditional withdrawal of the Iraqi troops from Kuwait. The USSR instantly became an intermediary between the United States and Iraq, as a direct talk between the two countries was not possible. By mid-February, it looked like a solution without a ground war was possible. Despite that, the Coalition air force continued to bombard Iraqi positions, causing further damage to both military and civilian targets. Not only that, but it was starting to intensify the raids, combining them with probing skirmishes with the Iraqi Army on the ground. The land invasion was undoubtedly drawing near.

Chapter 6 – The First Battles in the Desert

The destruction and casualties caused by the Coalition bombings were enough to convince the Iraqi leadership to seek a peaceful solution to the ongoing crisis. It was clear to everyone that the Iraqi Army, despite the boasting and propaganda on both sides, was no match for the US-led Coalition force. However, no matter how devastating the aerial campaign turned out to be, Saddam and the Ba'ath regime was not ready to accept an unconditional surrender. To achieve that goal, the US had to flex its military muscles even harder and hit the Iraqis on the ground.

However, in a rather surprising turn of events, it was actually the Iraqis who first engaged in land combat. During the last days of January, while the Coalition bombing was reaching its peak, Saddam and his military advisors started forming a plan of attack on Saudi territory. They realized that this prolonged bombardment would only worsen their military positions since the Iraqi air defense wasn't capable of dealing enough casualties to the US forces to turn the Gulf War into a new Vietnam. Thus, they chose to attack the small Saudi city of Khafji. It is located about twelve miles (twenty kilometers) southeast of the Kuwaiti-Saudi border, on the shores of the Persian Gulf. Due to its closeness, it was in the range of Iraqi artillery; thus, its population, at the time roughly numbering about 15,000 people, were evacuated when the war started. Iraqi generals were likely aware of that fact. For them, it was a rather suitable target void of possible civilian casualties that would further vilify the Iraqis in the eyes of the world. The strategic position of Khafji also made it an alluring target. The city was located on the only junction of the coastal road linking Saudi Arabia with Kuwait to the north and Bahrain, Qatar, the UAE, and Oman to the south. Even more important was the nearby Wafra oil field, which was jointly exploited by the Kuwaitis and the Saudis. Another factor made Khafji viable prey for the Iraqi generals. It was defended mostly by Saudi and Qatar troops, which were undoubtedly a much more desirable opponent for the Iraqi soldiers than the US forces.

After several days of preparation, the plan was set. The Iraqi Army was to attack with mechanized and armored divisions on the land, separated in three columns, while being aided by special forces attacking by the sea. The attack came on the night of January 29th, at about 8 p.m. local time. The Coalition command was surprised by this bold action, even though its reconnaissance teams reported the possibility of an Iraqi movement. The first to attack was the westernmost column, which encountered the lightly armed US troops. This assault was repulsed only when the Coalition air force, most notably the A-10 Tank Killer aircraft and the AC-130 gunships, came in to support. A similar scenario unfolded in the center column as well, where, once again, the aerial support defended the lightly armed US soldiers. However, the easternmost column, which was traveling next to the shoreline, proved to be the most determined. After enduring the bombing of the Coalition air force, it managed to enter the city just after midnight, as the Saudi defenders were ordered to retreat. The Iraqi Army fulfilled its initial goal, essentially achieving victory in the initial stages of the battle.

Nevertheless, it was a pyrrhic victory. The Iraqi troops suffered heavy losses, especially in the number of vehicles lost. The hardest hit was the Iraqi naval force. The fourth column, the commando attack from the sea, was quickly spotted by the Coalition ships. The small Iraqi speedboats were no match for the superior Coalition frigates and cruisers. Some were sunk, while others began to flee. Over the next couple of days, the Coalition vessels and aircraft, led by the British navy, continued to hunt down Iraqi patrol boats and smaller ships. Some tried to escape to the Iranians, but only one managed to do so. By February 2nd, the Iraqi Navy ceased to exist as a fighting force, as it was almost completely destroyed. Apart from heavy losses, this initial conflict also showcased two aspects of the war that were to become underlying themes in all future ground conflicts between the Coalition and Iraqi forces. One was that aerial superiority was a crucial factor for the Coalition to achieve its ground victories. The second was that the friendly fire was as much of a threat to the Coalition soldiers as the Iraqis were. The US military lost eleven men and two APCs because of misidentification and miscommunication.

A US LAV-AT destroyed by friendly fire in the Battle of Khafji.
Source: https://commons.wikimedia.org

Regardless, the Iraqis were holding the city since the early hours of January 30th. The following day, the effort to recapture Khafji began. The attack was spearheaded by the Saudi troops, which were aided by a Qatari tank division. The US forces provided artillery and aerial support. However, during the first day, the Iraqis managed to hold on to their positions, but they were once again affected by heavy casualties due to the attacks from the air. The Coalition bombers didn't only target the Iraqi troops in the city but also every unit spotted near the Kuwaiti-Saudi border. The plan was to stop any reinforcements and supplies from reaching the troops in Khafji. Thanks to their complete aerial superiority, this task was fulfilled, and the following day, the Saudi forces renewed their attacks. The second attack was more successful, managing to destroy and capture parts of the occupying Iraqi troops, who, by the end of the day, ended up being surrounded. By that time, the morale of the Iraqi soldiers had fallen. When the Coalition attack resumed on February 1st, most of them surrendered without a fight. After only two days of Iraqi occupation, Khafji was back under Saudi control.

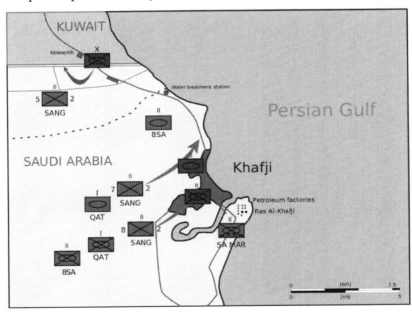

Battle of Khafji. Source: https://commons.wikimedia.org

The result of the Battle of Khafji was a clear military victory for the Coalition. Over the course of just four days, hundreds of Iraqis were killed or captured, the Iraqi Navy was basically obliterated, and the Iraqi Army lost hundreds of tanks and APCs. Most of these losses were caused from enemy aircraft, which severely damaged the morale of the Iraqis. A captured Iraqi soldier said that the Coalition air force caused more damage to his unit in half an hour than the Iranians did during the whole eight years of the Iran-Iraq War. The Iraqi commanders on the ground shared the sentiment, as one of the generals commented that "the mother was killing her children," alluding to Saddam's "mother of all battles" phrase. In contrast to those heavy losses, the combined casualties of the US and the Saudis were about 100 men wounded and killed, with only a handful of vehicles lost. More importantly for them, the Iraqi plan failed, as they didn't manage to lure them into further ground combat. However, the harsh reality didn't stop Saddam from proclaiming victory in this skirmish. He used that notion in both his domestic and international propaganda, trying to gain political points and raise the morale of his soldiers.

The success of the Ba'ath propaganda regarding the Battle of Khafji was at best limited. Internationally, only a few Arab countries welcomed the clash as an Iraqi victory, while most of the world saw nothing good coming from it. More worryingly, the domestic reach of the Khafji story spin was only marginally successful. With daily bombardments and heavy military losses, the citizens of Iraq weren't convinced the war was going in their favor. The Iraqi soldiers seemed even less confident, while the upper Iraqi command started having doubts. Thus, when in the following days the Coalition bombing continued to make Iraqi soil tremble, the Ba'ath leadership was becoming more open to negotiations. Therefore, when the Soviets sent their envoy to Baghdad on February 12th, Saddam's regime was ready to compromise for peace. Only three days later, the Iraqi leadership stepped up with an offer. If the American and other Western forces withdrew from the region, Iraq would be willing to deal with UN Resolution 660, which demanded the immediate and unconditional withdrawal of Iraq, while the future of the country was to be decided by the Arab nations, including Kuwait. Another condition was for the Israeli troops to withdraw from Arab lands. President Bush Sr. dismissed the offer as a hoax and an attempt to divide the Coalition allies. Regardless, the Soviets saw it as a starting offer, something to be explored in the hope of achieving a more peaceful resolution.

In the following days, both President Gorbachev and Tariq Aziz, the Iraqi minister of foreign affairs, came out with their peace proposals. Rather similar in nature, both of their ideas revolved around achieving the ceasefire and withdrawal of Iraqi troops from Kuwait while still linking the peace to the Arab-Israeli conflict. For the US, as well as the Arab Coalition leaders, this was unacceptable. Iraqi withdrawal had to be unconditional. Furthermore, Bush Sr. and his office felt that by allowing the Iraqis to simply retreat would leave the resolution of the conflict rather unclear and ambiguous. In their point of view, that would leave enough room for Saddam to politically exploit the outcome of the war. For some members of Bush's Cabinet, the only successful end of Desert Storm was if Iraq suffered an indisputable military defeat and was penalized for its aggression. For that reason, some more aggressive members of the US government hoped that Iraq wouldn't yield just from the bombing. They wanted the war to expand onto the ground. And while the US held firm on its non-negotiable position, the Soviets talked with the Iraqi representatives to try to find a compromise, hoping to avoid the conflict from broadening even more.

By February 21st, Gorbachev, backed up by Tariq Aziz, proposed a new plan. It called for the unconditional withdrawal of the Iraqi troops, in accordance with Resolution 660, followed by the ceasefire and lifting of all sanctions when two-thirds of the Iraqi soldiers left Kuwait. The war was to be ended with the nullification of all UN resolutions when the withdrawal was complete. However, in contrast to the diplomatic offers, Iraq's behavior on the ground spoke differently. Saddam was giving warmongering speeches, while the soldiers began burning Kuwaiti oil fields and supposedly killing Kuwaiti civilians. Therefore, the latest Soviet plan was once again rejected by the Bush administration, which, on the following day, sent out its own ultimatum. Iraq had 24 hours, until February 23rd, 5:00 p.m. GMT, to begin their withdrawal from Kuwait, which was to be finished within seven days. Furthermore, Iraq was to return full control over the territory to the Kuwaiti government, release all prisoners, and give up military control over the Kuwaiti air and land to the Coalition. In return, the Coalition was not to fire upon the retreating Iraqi forces. This ultimatum only sped up the Soviet Union's attempts to avoid a ground war.

A picture of burning Kuwaiti oil fields (March 1991). Source: https://commons.wikimedia.org

In a matter of hours, Gorbachev came out with a new plan. The Iraqi withdrawal would begin within a day of the ceasefire agreement, and it would be completed in three weeks. The UN resolutions would be annulled after the withdrawal occurred. Early on February 23rd, Tariq Aziz openly accepted this plan. However, Bush Sr. was adamant. The Iraqi Army was to begin pulling out of Kuwait in a matter of hours. The Soviet president tried to convince his US colleague through a phone call to push back the deadline for another 24 hours, as an acceptable compromise was only a day away. These efforts were futile. President Bush wasn't budging, and he had the support of other major members of the Coalition. This left US-USSR relations somewhat strained, as Gorbachev stated that the Americans were more interested in an armed resolution than in a peaceful diplomatic solution, a remark not far from the truth. In the end, the Iraqi leaders didn't fulfill the US ultimatum, and the Coalition wasn't giving them more time to reconsider. Thus, on February 23rd, at 6:00 p.m. GMT, President Bush greenlighted the beginning of the land operations in Iraq. This military operation was codenamed "Desert Sabre."

In the days before the full Coalition ground offensive, while the diplomats and politicians were talking and negotiating, both armies prepared for the inevitable clash. The Coalition forces continued to bombard the Iraqi positions, softening their defenses, knocking out their equipment, and lowering the morale of the Iraqi soldiers. Furthermore, Coalition ground troops began skirmishing with Iraqi soldiers, preventing their reconnaissance teams from observing the Coalition positions. This was only furthered between February 15th and 20th when several US units attacked the Iraqi positions along the Iraq-Kuwait border. However, these attacks were limited feint operations that were designed to make the Iraqis think that the main Coalition invasion would take place near the tripoint of Iraq, Kuwait, and Saudi Arabia. The ploy was helped by the fact that it was a natural invasion route. Thus, after limited clashes, the US troops returned to their original positions, while the Iraqi army focused on defending that sector of the front. The goal was to draw the Iraqi forces from the western portions of the front, where the US VII Army Corps would lead the main Coalition attack. These incursive actions warned the Iraqi high command that an attack was imminent. Thus, they began preparing their defenses.

Apart from the conventional tactics, like laying down mines and fortifying their positions, the Ba'ath generals also decided to use Kuwaiti oil fields as a part of their natural defenses. They began spilling the oil, burning it in an attempt to create large fire lakes and thick clouds to impede the Coalition advancement and forcing them to enter predetermined "death zones" created by these obstacles. Even if the fires were to run out, the oil residue, mixed with tar and sand, would leave a layer of so-called "tarcrete," which would jam up the tracks of the Coalition tanks. However, it should be noted that not all of the several hundred burning Kuwaiti oil fields should be blamed on the Iraqis. About fifty of them were lit up by Coalition bombings, which were targeting nearby Iraqi units, before mid-February 1991. The Iraqis also dumped large quantities of crude oil just off the shores of Kuwait in the Persian Gulf. They hoped it would cause problems for the expected Coalition naval assault. These tactics were highly controversial worldwide, as many saw them more as an intentional ecological catastrophe than a viable military strategy. From the Iraqi perspective, this tactic made sense because it was also damaging the Kuwaiti oil industry, which was one of the reasons the war even began. Regardless of both the ecological and infrastructural damage, the Iraqi Army was waiting for the imminent attack of the Coalition forces, which finally arrived at 4:00 a.m. local time on February 24th.

The overall plan of the attack was rather simple. The eastern flank, consisting of Saudi, Egyptian, Syrian, and other Arab troops, helped by the US 1st Marine Expeditionary Force, was to push north directly into Kuwait. They were under the command of Saudi Prince Khalid bin Sultan. The reason why the Arab forces were tasked with liberating Kuwait was that they refused to fight on Iraqi territory, limiting the range of their actions to only up to the Kuwait-Iraq border. The main attack on the center of the front was given to the US VII Army Corps, under the command of Lieutenant-General Fred Franks Jr., which was aided by the British troops. Their goal was to flank the Iraqi forces in Kuwait and encircle them. It was expected that the units attacking this sector would encounter the fiercest resistance, as most of the infamous Republican Guard was located on their path. The western flank was left to the US XVIII Airborne Corps, which was aided by the French troops. Commanded by Lieutenant-General Gary Luck, it was tasked with blocking possible reinforcements the Iraqi Army would send to the south and would have to push the deepest into enemy territory. The success of the plan, which is ascribed to US General Schwarzkopf, hinged on speed. The Coalition forces had to move quickly and relentlessly to avoid being bogged down in prolonged combat, which could lead to higher casualties than needed.

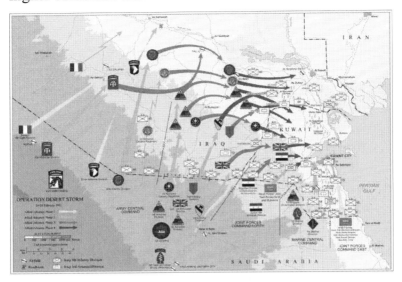

Plan and execution of Operation Desert Storm. Source: https://commons.wikimedia.org

The implementation of Schwarzkopf's plan was more than swift. On the eastern flank, the Arab and US forces moved into Kuwait, first encountering the Iraqi units that attacked Khafji. Unexpectedly, these troops showed little resistance. It seemed their battle morale had dissipated over the weeks of heavy bombardment, combined by the fact that most of the soldiers felt abandoned by Baghdad. Two captured Iraqi officers even stated that they were left without any orders for about two weeks. The extent of how low Iraqi morale was can be illustrated by the US assessment that some 150,000 troops deserted even before the main ground operations had begun. Because of that, the Coalition push into Kuwait proved to be quick and mostly painless, as most of the Iraqis simply surrendered at the first sight of the advancing troops. The fact that they mostly encountered fellow Arabs on the other side possibly made their decision to surrender easier. And as the Arab-US troops advanced on the eastern front, they began forming the anvil for the VII Army Corps hammer, which was breaking through the center of the battlefield. The major attacks on that part of the battlefield were preceded by short artillery barrages, in which more than 10,000 shells were fired to pummel the Iraqi defenses.

The breakthrough in the center of this front was spearheaded by the famous 1st US Infantry Division, the "Big Red One," which wiped out the Iraqi division that opposed it. On the western flank of the "Big Red One," armored and cavalry divisions pushed on, swiveling toward the center. Those were to join the 1st Infantry Division in their primary goal, hunting down the Republican Guard that was stationed in the back of the Iraqi defense lines as a strategic reserve. On the eastern flank of the central front, the British 1st Armored Division, known as the "Desert Rats," pushed through the breach created by the Big Red One. It was racing toward Kuwait in order to protect the VII Army Corps' push toward the Republican Guard. The Iraqi commanders were taken by surprise by the overall actions of the VII Army Corps. First of all, they expected the main attack to happen on the western flank, where the armored and cavalry division poured in. Furthermore, they assumed its main goal was to push toward Kuwait immediately instead of driving deeper into Iraqi territory to face the Republican Guard. When they realized the main intent of the Coalition attack, the Guard began to reposition. Among those units were three elite divisions, the Medina, the Hammurabi, and the Tawakalna. Their main goal was to stop the VII Army Corps from breaching through to the Iraqi rear positions.

In the western sector, the XVIII Airborne Corps proved to be the most successful. In the center, the US 101st Airborne Division pushed about 93 miles (150 kilometers) inside Iraqi territory with a massive airlift involving 400 helicopters. There, they established a forward operating base named Cobra. From there, they pushed 60 miles (96 kilometers) farther north toward the Euphrates River. There, it cut off Highway 8, the main road connecting central and southern Iraq. On their western flank was the French 6th Light Armoured Division, which was aided by the US 82nd Airborne

Division. They rushed through the desert to take the Al-Salman Air Base and protect the left flank of the 101st Airborne Division. On the right flank, the US 24th Mechanized Infantry Division, reinforced by the US 3rd Armored Cavalry Regiment, pushed north to meet up with the 101st in the area of the Cobra base before turning eastward to aid the VII Army Corps in its attack on the Republican Guard. The XVIII Airborne Corps managed to fulfill its initial goals ahead of time, prompting General Schwarzkopf to speed up overall operations a few hours ahead of schedule. The unexpected swiftness of the Coalition breakthrough was achieved mostly due to the lack of Iraqi morale. On top of that, the allies had a clear technological advantage, as the Iraqi tanks were no match for the British and US counterparts, while the aerial support further weakened the Iraqi positions.

Saddam Hussein himself further hindered Iraqi resistance. He was more concerned with preserving his regime than holding their positions in the south. Because of that, the Iraqi leader held back some of the more important units and was unwilling to risk losing his most trusted Republican Guard. Furthermore, if there was ever a time when the Iraqi troops needed at least some air support, it was at the time of this Coalition attack. Unfortunately for them, Saddam kept most of the planes grounded. With such orders, the Iraqi generals were unable to mount a more serious attempt of defense, while the troops on the ground felt as if they were being sacrificed. Even worse, Saddam wanted to withdraw as many soldiers as possible to the north in an attempt to reinforce his own positions. Still, with Highway 8 being cut off, this was not a viable option. However, as the Coalition forces pushed through southern Iraq during February 25th, things began to change slightly. The first Iraqi units started pulling out of Kuwait that night, while, simultaneously, troops on the central front began showing slightly stiffer opposition. Nonetheless, the future of the Iraqi troops looked dim. By the end of that day, the Coalition basically cut off the Iraqi Army in Kuwait and the Basra region from the northern regions of Iraq.

Achieving that in such a short time, within just two days, the allied forces were actually exceeding the goals given to them by the high command. The speed with which they broke through the initial defenses of the Iraqi Army surprised even the most senior officers of the Coalition, let alone the rest of the world. Witnessing just how much the Coalition was overpowered in contrast with the Iraqi Army, it was clear that Saddam lacked the power to resist the Coalition attack. However, it didn't mean that the Iraqis would go down without a fight, at least when it came to the ever-loyal Republican Guard.

Chapter 7 – Iraqi Defeat and the Aftermath of the War

After just about 48 hours, the Coalition forces managed to push deep into Iraqi territory, almost seamlessly. Using their superior technology and air support, the allied units managed to break what little fighting spirit the Iraqi Army had left after weeks of heavy bombardments. Most of the regular troops began piling up around Basra, hoping for a miracle since the reinforcement from the north clearly wasn't coming. It was clear that the liberation of Kuwait was within reach, leaving only the secondary target of the Coalition troops to be achieved. That was to destroy Saddam's loyal elite guards.

Destroyed Iraqi T-62 (left) and the US artillery firing upon the Iraqi positions (right) – February 1991. Source: https://commons.wikimedia.org

By the early morning of February 26th, the US VII Army Corps finally caught up to the Republican Guard. The first unit they encountered was the Tawakalna Division in a tank battle that lasted for much of the day. The Iraqis dug in, providing a much stiffer resistance than any previous enemy the VII Army Corps had encountered. The Tawakalna proved its elite status, at least when compared to other Iraqi divisions. It held out for much of the day, though it was assisted by poor visibility from the weather conditions. In the end, even the Republican Guard proved to be no match for the US and British forces. Their T-72s were outgunned on the ground and by the Coalition air force, which began picking them off as soon as the weather started to improve. By the end of the 26th, the Tawakalna Division broke and began to withdraw. The Medina Division, another elite unit of the Guard, which was aided by a regular Iraqi Army division, tried to cover their retreat, to no avail. The air raid picked off most of what was left of the Tawakalna. However, parts of the elite Iraqi division survived to fight another day, even though its capabilities were significantly diminished.

During the same day the Tawakalna Division suffered their defeat, Iraqi forces farther south in Kuwait began preparing for an evacuation. The Arab and US troops reached the city itself during the day, while the Iraqis began fleeing. However, remnants of the Iraqi 3rd Armored Division, which were veterans of both the Iran-Iraq War and the 1973 Arab-Israeli Yom Kippur War, decided to hold their ground. It seems they decided to put up a stiff resistance in the hopes of buying some time for their fleeing comrades. Their efforts proved to be futile in more than one way. The Iraqis tried to dig in, relying on what was left of their tanks and APCs (armored personnel carriers), but once again, they proved to be an inadequate match for the more modern equipment heralded by the US troops that were spearheading the attack. Regardless of that, the Iraqi veterans showed stiff resistance, as they were finally defeated only during the next day, making their last stand near the Kuwait International Airport. With that, the liberation of Kuwait was technically finished, and the main objective of the Coalition was achieved. However, this accomplishment was largely tainted by the events that transpired mostly during the night between February 26th and 27th. As the veterans of the Iraqi 3rd Armored Division fought hard in the city to provide at least some time for the other retreating

Iraqi troops, their comrades gathered up a large group of mostly civilian vehicles and began their flight north.

They headed up on Highway 80 from Kuwait to Basra. It wasn't long before their flight started resembling traffic congestion. Of course, the Coalition planes spotted them, and on the orders of the high command, they began attacking them. First, they opened fire on the head and the tail of the fleeing column, boxing the rest in between. Then, over the course of more than ten hours in a series of repeated attacks, the Coalition pilots proceeded to basically massacre the Iraqis. By the morning, only charred debris and burnt bodies were left, dotting miles of the road. This caused an uproar among the international public, as many saw it as excessive use of force. The Iraqis were withdrawing, mostly unarmed, prompting some to argue that these attacks violated the Geneva Convention, which bans the killing of soldiers who are out of combat. Others added that there were civilians among the military personnel, which was never completely confirmed. The US command responded by claiming that they were simply destroying the Iraqi military equipment, which could have been used in future combat. Other US officers also added that the killed Iraqis were just "a bunch of rapists, murderers and thugs" who were trying to escape. The number of casualties was also a matter of debate, as some army officials claimed that most of the Iraqis abandoned their vehicles when the attacks started. Regardless, the event on what became known as the "Highway of Death" left a bitter taste to many international observers.

A later picture of the "Highway of Death" with a T-55 in the front (April 1991). Source: https://commons.wikimedia.org

However, those events had little effects on the other Coalition troops. On the next day, February 27th, the advancing US forces of the VII Army Corps, led by the US 1st Armored Division, engaged the Medina Division, which was reinforced with minor remnants of the Tawakalna and regular Iraqi Army brigades. Once again, the Iraqi elites justified their reputation. They chose to dig in on the high ground behind a ridge, giving them strong defensive positions with an element of surprise. The advancing American units were unable to see them clearly before passing the ridgeline. Thanks to their tactical choices, as well as their strong will to fight, the Medina Division put up what was most likely the fiercest resistance of the war, even managing to shoot down some of the US aircraft. In the clash that became known as the Battle of Medina Ridge, they held their positions for the entire day. Yet, once again, their equipment proved to be no match for the US artillery and air force. Even the American tanks proved to be too much of a challenge for them simply because they outranged the generation older Soviet T-72s that the Guard used. Thus, by the end of the day, the Medina

Division was defeated as well, suffering significant losses, especially in tanks and APCs.

At the same time as the Battle of Medina Ridge, another major clash occurred in the relative vicinity. The US 1st Infantry Division, aided by other American and British armored and artillery divisions, engaged a mishmash of Iraqi armored and infantry divisions that had survived thus far. Even some other remnants of the Tawakalna Division were present. The Iraqis were trying to fortify their positions, as they had no other viable options in their attempts to resist the invading forces. Once again, the Iraqi troops showed some will to resist but to no avail. Their dug-in tanks were easy targets for the Coalition aerial bombardment and artillery. As the day progressed, their resistance was slowly broken, and the Iraqi troops began surrendering. By the end of the day, the Coalition forces marked another important victory. It became known as the Battle of Norfolk, as it was located in a desert area near the Iraq-Kuwait border that the Coalition command called Objective Norfolk. The Iraqi Army lost a large chunk of its fighting force and a substantial number of vehicles and equipment. The exact quantities of both deployed and destroyed Iraqi tanks are still debated, as historians are still arguing which of the two significant battles of the day, the Battle of Medina Ridge or the Battle of Norfolk, hold the title for the largest tank battle of the Gulf War.

A dug-in Iraqi T-72 at the Battle of Norfolk. Source: https://commons.wikimedia.org

Farther north, the US 24th Mechanized Infantry Division followed the Euphrates River eastward, toward the city of Basra. On February 27th, it engaged the Republican Guard forces of the Al-Faw Division, which was aided by smaller detachments from the Nebuchadnezzar and Hammurabi Divisions near the Lake Hammar. The Al-Faw stood valiantly against the 24th Division, giving it the toughest resistance since the division had crossed into Iraq. However, like all the other battles that day, those Iraqi efforts were futile. Most of the Al-Faw Division was rendered combat ineffective, while parts of the Hammurabi and the Nebuchadnezzar Divisions fled back toward Basra. While the US 24th Mechanized Infantry Division was closing down on the city, the US 101st and 82nd Airborne Divisions were locking down the escape routes along the Euphrates River, as well as protecting the back of the Coalition forces. Effectively, by the end of the day, what was left of the Iraqi forces in the south was confined to the area around Basra. The Iraqi Army suffered significant losses and was almost completely surrounded in the so-called "Basra pocket." The only viable escape routes were north of Lake Hammar, which was along the Shatt al-Arab and Tigris Rivers.

At this point, the political and military leadership of the Coalition diverged in opinions. The leading US generals believed their secondary objective, rendering the Republican Guard ineffective, was not yet completely fulfilled. The Iraqi elite units did suffer substantial losses, mostly in terms of equipment, with the Tawakalna and the Al-Faw Divisions supposedly ceasing to exist as fighting forces. However, for the US generals, including General Schwarzkopf, this meant that the job was only partially done. In their eyes, the Guard was still a viable threat in the region. On the other hand, politicians, most notably President Bush Sr. himself, felt the goal of the Coalition was attained. The Iraqi Army was expelled from Kuwait, while the brunt of their fighting force and equipment were destroyed. Combined with horrific images of the Highway of Death and other similar scenes of destruction, it was enough for the international, as well as the US, public to doubt if the Coalition was going for the overkill. This was only furthered by the fact that the UN resolution tasked the Coalition with only liberating Kuwait, not destroying the Iraqi Army or toppling Saddam's regime. This prompted President Bush Sr. to declare a ceasefire at 8:00 a.m. on February 28th, exactly 100 hours since the official ground operations had begun.

This decision of the United States commander-in-chief spurred quite a bit of debate among the American public. One course of thought, more militaristic in nature, saw it as a mistake. Saddam's Ba'ath regime was not only left in charge of Iraq, but it was also allowed to retain too much military power. Others thought it was the right choice since the UN mission was fulfilled, and the Iraqi Army was undoubtedly defeated. This discussion was brought up again after the US invaded Iraq for the second time in 2003. However, in late February 1991, President Bush Sr. had to consider both the diplomatic climate and his own political legacy. By ending the war when he did, the US president prevented unwarranted Iraqi casualties, which would have almost certainly led to international disapproval. It would have tainted both the impressive American victory and his political career. Furthermore, if the US Army decided to continue the war to topple Saddam, the Coalition would have most likely fractured. The Arab members were undoubtedly against the American intervention in what were internal affairs of Iraq. Thus, President Bush Sr. saw only one right choice, leaving both his own and the face of the United States unblemished.

The Iraqi government was eager to accept the ceasefire, and the war was considered to be finished, even though no official document had been signed. It was agreed that the formal peace negotiations were to be held on March 2nd at Safwan Air Base, just a few miles from the Iraq-Kuwait border on the road toward Basra. However, while the talks were ongoing, the Hammurabi Division attempted to withdraw from the Basra pocket toward Baghdad, passing between the Rumaila oil field and Lake Hammar. On its path was the US 24th Mechanized Infantry Division, which had no intention to let them through. Without following any orders from the Iraqi high command, the Hammurabi soldiers opened gunfire on the US troops that tried to block their escape. That provoked a fierce reaction from the American forces. The long column of the retreating Iraqi troops was first enclosed in a killing zone, after which they were subjugated to the systemic destruction from both the US ground forces and their artillery and aircraft support. The Hammurabi Division was devastated. It lost several hundred vehicles, with over 700 soldiers killed and 3,000 captured. The Battle of Rumaila, as this event became known, sparked another round of controversies among the observers of the war.

Charred remains of the Iraqi vehicles after the Battle of Rumaila (March 1991). Source: https://commons.wikimedia.org

The question was raised if the 24th Division had justification for unleashing such destruction, even though the Iraqis had fired first. Some even questioned the reason the US unit moved into the way of the retreating Iraqis in the first place, as this took place during the armistice. Especially dubious were the actions of the US soldiers, which were against all rules of civilized combat. Most of the Hammurabi Division wasn't battle-ready, with many of their tanks and other equipment loaded up on transportation vehicles; attacking them was the equivalent of shooting an unarmed man. Even worse, there were reports of US soldiers firing upon wounded, medics, and surrendering Iraqi soldiers. The extent of the violence was shockingly unjustifiable, proving that President Bush Sr. made the right call. If the war continued, it was likely that more similar events would have happened, as American soldiers were more than eager to punish "the evil Iraqis." Of course, this incident caused some friction at the negotiating table, but the Iraqi government had little choice.

The only way both the Ba'ath regime and Iraq as a whole would survive was to agree on the terms given to them by the Coalition command. Thus, on March 3rd, 1991, in Safwan, the hostilities were officially ended as the two sides signed the ceasefire. The Iraqi side agreed on the terms set by the Coalition. Both sides were to exchange prisoners. Iraq had reportedly captured 41 soldiers, some of whom later claimed to have been savagely tortured and beaten in the hopes of extracting information about the Coalition plans. On the other side, the Coalition troops were holding more than 60,000 Iraqis, most of whom seemed to have been dealt with in accordance with the 1949 Geneva Convention. It was a shocking revelation to the Iraqi negotiator, who was unaware of just how extensive the Iraqi defeat was.

Furthermore, the Iraqi Army was to give precise information on the minefields it had laid in the region, most notably in Kuwait. Apart from that, a temporary ceasefire line was drawn to avoid any new unwarranted clashes like the 24th and Hammurabi Divisions had. The Iraqis were also banned from using fixed-wing aircraft, but after their negotiator pleaded, they were permitted the use of helicopters. The Iraqi government argued that with the substantial destruction of the Iraqi infrastructure, helicopters were needed to facilitate movement across the country. Iraq was also ordered to allow the UN representatives on their territory. They were to oversee the removal of chemical and biological weapons, as well as the ballistic missiles with ranges over 93 miles (150 kilometers). The Iraqi government also had to accept and implement all of the UN resolutions concerning the Gulf War and the issue of Kuwait. At the same time, Iraq had to officially recognize the line of the Iraq-Kuwait border as defined under the 1963 agreement.

On top of that, the border between the two countries was demarcated with a demilitarized area, which protruded six miles (ten kilometers) into Iraq, while it was only half as large on the Kuwaiti side. Iraq was further ordered to release all Kuwaiti prisoners and detainees, return all the pillaged property, and pay reparation damages to Kuwait. In return, the UN was to lift its sanctions, which was desperately needed by the Iraqi civilian population. All in all, the Safwan accord was less of a negotiation and more of an Iraqi surrender, a fact that was only confirmed when one looked at the state of the battlefield after the initial ceasefire was proclaimed. As Saddam and his regime accepted the imposed conditions, the Coalition troops slowly began to withdraw from the region. The Coalition victory was celebrated, or at least praised, across most of the world. However, Iraqi propaganda represented it differently. As it was still under the unchallenged control of Saddam Hussein, it informed the Iraqi citizens that the peace was only achieved because their soldiers had fought valiantly, forcing the Coalition to ask for a ceasefire. Thus, the Ba'ath regime proclaimed its triumph in the so-called "mother of all battles."

Demilitarized zone between Iraq and Kuwait (left) and Kuwaiti civilians celebrating with Coalition soldiers over their liberation from the Iraqis (right). Source: https://commons.wikimedia.org

Of course, most of the Iraqi people were aware that this "news" was mere propaganda ploy. Thousands of disgruntled soldiers were returning home, with full knowledge of just how terrifying their defeat was. Almost all the civilians felt the devastation caused by the Coalition bombardment, and even more of them were affected by the UN economic blockade. The dissatisfaction piled up throughout the Gulf War, but there was nowhere it could be expressed, as the government kept strict control over both the media and the population. Thus, when the war was finished, with even Saddam's most loyal troops and his government apparatus in disarray, local uprisings began rising up. The first flames of revolt lit up during March 1st near the city of Basra before spreading across Iraq. It wasn't a single centralized rebellion, headed by some organization or a leader, and it was not even backed by some broad ideology. It was a simple outburst of frustration among the Iraqi citizens across the country. The rebels were from various ethnic, social, and religious backgrounds. Among them were the long-oppressed Kurds in northern Iraq, the Shia Muslim majority oppressed by the Ba'ath minority, and the far-leftists. Even more worryingly for Saddam's regime was the fact that the rebellion was supported not only by demobilized Iraqi soldiers but also by active ones, making it also partially a military mutiny.

An Iraqi government tank destroyed by the rebels (March 1991).
Source: https://commons.wikimedia.org

The Ba'ath government had to act quickly if it wanted to reestablish its tight grip over Iraq, as the insurgents achieved some initial minor successes. The central Iraqi government lost control of several cities in southern and northern Iraq. The rebels expressed their frustration by both destroying symbols of the Ba'ath regime, like statues and buildings, but also by killing hundreds of Ba'ath officials, officers, and supporters. Saddam and his high officials didn't respond immediately, as they waited to finish the dealings with the Coalition. Thus, their counteroffensive began on March 7th, with the Republican Guard serving as the tip of the loyalist blade. However, the uprisings proved to be much tougher to extinguish than it would have been before the conflict. The Iraqi Army was not only divided but also severely lacking in equipment and vehicles due to the losses from the war. On the other side, the rebels weren't eager to back down. Their will to fight was only additionally fueled by US messages, which prompted them to liberate themselves from Saddam's dictatorship. President Bush Sr. and his Cabinet believed, or at least hoped, that the Iraqi people could finish off the Ba'ath regime for them, as their hands were tied from interfering directly in Iraqi internal matters.

US pamphlet representing Saddam Hussein as death (left) and Kurdish children playing with abandoned military equipment (right) – March 1991. Source: https://commons.wikimedia.org

To both their and the rebels' shock, the blade of nonintervention cut both sides. While the Coalition forces slowly withdrew from Iraq, the loyalist regime began suppressing the uprising. Their primary tools, to which the insurgents could hardly parry, were the Iraqi Army helicopters. Only a handful of them was destroyed during the war, and they were exempt from the Coalition's no-fly ban. Thus, they began to lead the aerial attacks on the defenseless rebels. They looked to the Americans for support, as they were the ones encouraging their revolt, but the US troops were unable to help them. It would be seen as interfering in Iraqi internal affairs. Therefore, the loyalists were left to massacre their compatriots across the country, while the Coalition could do little more than watch. The Ba'ath regime went on to murder not only the armed combatants of the rebellion but also defenseless civilians that supported them. However, despite their military superiority, the loyalists needed almost a full month to quell all the uprisings. It wasn't until April 5th, 1991, that the rebels were finally defeated, as this was the day that the Ba'ath government declared that it crushed all attempts of sedition, sabotage, and rioting in all Iraqi cities. Ironically, it was on that very same day that the UN adopted Resolution 788, in which it demanded the Ba'ath government stop its repression of the Kurd and Shia population in Iraq. By then, though, tens of thousands were already killed, and the rebel uprising had failed.

Despite the fact that the rebellions had been put down, the United States, Britain, and France established two no-fly zones without seeking an Iraqi agreement. Those zones covered the areas in the north and the south, where most of the uprisings took place. Furthermore, Iraq was forced to replace either allied troops or its own police with UN security in some cities that were part of the rebellion. Iraq objected to many of these decisions, somewhat rightfully claiming they were infringing on its sovereignty. Additionally, after the initial shock of defeat began wearing off and the Coalition troops began to return home, the Ba'ath government began to protest the UN inspectors coming to Iraq to oversee the dismantling of banned weapons and nuclear sites, even though it had agreed on it in the Safwan accord. Not only that, but it began interfering with their work, somewhat obstructing them in their jobs. The Iraqis claimed some of them were Western spies who took photographs and sent sensitive information to the US and Israel. These accusations were usually dismissed without any serious consequences, even though, in some cases, they proved to be partially true. Some of the American members of the UN teams sent the information gathered first to Washington before reporting it to the United Nations.

By early 1992, the last of the Coalition forces left Iraq, even though there were US troops still stationed in the region. Over the next couple of years, those American forces acted unilaterally when it was deemed necessary. Their ships and planes bombarded Iraq whenever the United States estimated the Iraqis were breaking some agreement or possibly jeopardizing others. For example, an Iraqi radar station was destroyed after an American plane detected being scanned by it. At other times, the US bombardment was aimed at Iraqi defenses and ballistic missile sites. The most unique of these punitive actions came in June 1993 when Washington approved 23 Tomahawk cruise missiles to be launched on Baghdad. It was in retaliation for a supposed Iraqi-sponsored assassination attempt on, by that time, former President George Bush Sr., who was visiting Kuwait in May of that year. Washington claimed that the attack was an act of self-defense, which would mean the UN Charter justified it. Nonetheless, for many, it was seen as the US breaching international law, especially since there were signs that the supposed assassination reports seemed to be fabricated. Even worse was the fact that those limited and precision-targeted raids still managed to hit civilian structures and cause further unnecessary casualties. The rest of the world did little more than protest to stop these bombings, while Iraq itself could not do anything significant on its own.

Furthermore, in the months and years following the Gulf War, the United Nations never fully retracted the trade embargo imposed on

Iraq. It was claimed that the Iraqi government never fully implemented the terms of the peace, accusations which cannot be disregarded as entirely false. Like the US, Saddam also had his own interpretations of the peace conditions, working in the gray areas that were left. Thus, the UN quite rightfully kept the imposed embargo on military equipment and imports of anything that could be used in war or weaponized. In contrast with that, Iraq was allowed to buy food, medicine, and other similar products it severely lacked. However, a problem arose from the fact that Iraq was still banned from exporting its crude oil. Because of such measures, the Iraqi government was unable to find funds to buy the necessary commodities, while the war and extended sanctions crippled its agriculture and industry. By early 1994, several international organizations warned that Iraq was heading toward famine. This forced the UN to partially lift the embargo on Iraqi oil exports, limiting it to a certain amount, while resources had to be used only for acquiring food and medicine. Despite that, civilian life in Iraq still remained hard and destitute. The reason behind both the prolonged sanctions and the occasional punitive bombardment was the underlying desire of the US to prompt the Iraqis to topple the Ba'ath regime.

The effect was quite the opposite, though. The regime was doing more or less fine, while it was the Iraqi civilians who suffered. It took another war in 2003 to finally depose Saddam and the Ba'ath regime, which was undertaken by the United States without UN approval. Coincidentally, it was only then that the embargo imposed on Iraq was totally lifted. However, Iraq never really recovered from the fate that was brought on by its invasion of Kuwait, as the suffering of the Iraqi civilians continues to this day.

Chapter 8 – Casualties, Consequences, and the Legacy of the Gulf War

To fully understand the story of the Gulf War, it is not enough to talk about the battles and bombings, why it happened, how it got resolved, and when it ended. It is vital to take a closer look at the outcome and ramifications of the conflict, as well as the image of the war that is engraved in our minds today. Only then will the picture of the war be complete, as well as one's comprehension of the event in its fullest.

When it comes to understanding wars, one of the most important questions raised is one of casualties. That portion of the Gulf War remains rather controversial but also very illustrative. The Coalition forces in total had about 380 killed in action, with around 800 more who were wounded. Considering the number of troops involved, these were surprisingly small numbers, making it one of the most successful combat campaigns in history. However, the idealized picture is somewhat tainted by the percentage of friendly fire deaths. Out of the 146 American soldiers killed in action during the war, there were at least 35 confirmed cases of so-called "blue-on-blue" deaths. That is above 20% of the total US losses. The number of wounded American soldiers caused by friendly fire is even higher. The most severe act of "blue-on-blue" fire occurred on February 26th in the battle between the US VII Army Corps and the Tawakalna Division. No less than 57 American soldiers were injured by friendly fire, even though there were no fatalities. If that wasn't enough, there was a high rate of accidents among the Coalition troops, with a couple of hundred casualties of various nationalities. In the end, it proved that accidents, illness, and friendly fire took more allied lives than the Iraqi Army. Apart from the listed Coalition casualties, it should be noted that during the initial Iraqi invasion and occupation, Kuwait suffered several hundred military deaths and more than 1,000 civilian casualties.

In comparison to that, Iraq paid a much heftier toll. The exact number is unknown, as not even the Iraqi government had precise information. The media and certain experts and army officials of the time estimated that the Iraqi Army suffered about 200,000 killed in action. These numbers were significantly lowered, with most trusted evaluations ranging from about 25,000 to 35,000, with roughly an additional 75,000 wounded. The estimates of the Iraqi civilian deaths range from a rather conservative number of 3,500 upward to 15,000. The number of Iraqi casualties grows significantly higher when the uprisings are added to the final tally. According to various approximations, the number of casualties ranges from about 130,000 to 250,000 casualties when killed, wounded, and missing are all added up. Out of these, about 25,000 to 35,000 were unarmed civilian fatalities. The situation in which Iraq found itself only made its suffering worse. Their infrastructure was devastated, famine was spreading, and their healthcare system was collapsing, causing tens of thousands more deaths in the aftermath of the war. That led to an estimated 205,000 Iraqi deaths from direct and indirect consequences of war. In addition to the casualties, there were up to 1.8 million refugees, mostly Kurds and Shia minorities. They began fleeing the country in high numbers after the uprising was quelled. Running away from Saddam's oppression, they mostly fled to Turkey and Iran.

Seeing how much Iraq suffered from the war, both in casualties and destruction, many Western observers were surprised by Saddam's proclamation of victory. At the very least, they saw it as a propaganda ploy or his own personal delusions. In the grand scheme of things, there is no doubt that Iraq was defeated in the Gulf War, making Saddam's declaration almost laughable. However, for him and his Ba'ath high officials, the war wasn't as disastrous as it could have been. For the regime, which in no small degree went into the war to remain in power, their main goal was achieved. The Ba'ath Party, with Saddam at its head, not only stayed at the helm of Iraq but even tightened their grip. During the uprisings, they dealt with the parts of the Iraqi population who posed the most threat to the regime. Furthermore, the regular Iraqi Army, which had begun losing its faith in the government since the Iran-Iraq War, was decimated. It lost its strength for a possible organized coup. At the same time, the ever-loyal Republican Guard gained in might when compared to the regular Iraqi Army. Yet, the devastating results of the war did change Saddam's rule. The popularity of his regime and the Ba'ath Party was falling, forcing him to turn more toward the countryside tribal groups that were loyal only to him.

Saddam Hussein in 1998 (left) and the Iraqi flag with added Islamic phrase "The God is great," which was in use from 1991 to 2004. Source: https://commons.wikimedia.org

From those tribes, Saddam recruited people to serve him in the security services, military, government, and bureaucratic apparatus, making sure that he was surrounded by only loyal Iraqis.

Furthermore, the regime began rebuilding and forming new security agencies and intelligence networks, creating a tight and overlapping system to protect it from internal threats. The most vital parts of Saddam's security, those key positions in security and intelligence organizations, were given to his own family members. Apart from the changes in the regime's structure, the ideology of it was changing as well. The pan-Arab nationalism of the Ba'ath Party was largely abandoned. This was partially because Saddam had failed to fulfill his self-proclaimed role as an Arab unifier. Even worse was the fact that most of the Arab world turned against Iraq in its clash with the rest of the world instead of supporting it. Thus, the idea of pan-Arab unity seemed as only wishful thinking for both the common Iraqis as well as the Ba'ath leadership, including Saddam himself. So, the regime instead turned toward Islam as the basis of its ideology. In his speeches, Saddam started to use religious rhetoric, sometimes even depicting himself as a messiah or representative of God. The result of the war on the Iraqi government and society was its shifting from modernity and Arab nationalism toward more traditional and conservative ideas and organizations that were based in Islam and tribalism.

On the other hand, the United States celebrated its victory not only over Iraq but also over its fear of Vietnam. For more than fifteen years after its infamous defeat in Southeast Asia, the American public was very cautious about getting involved in any new wars or interventions. Both the public and the government were afraid of making the same mistakes again. However, after seeing how smoothly they won against the supposedly fourth largest army of the world, their self-confidence grew. Not only was the victory swift and with minimal casualties, but it also wasn't a tremendous burden on the US budget. Unlike the Vietnam War, where the US was both the main fighting force and the main financer, in the Gulf War, Saudi Arabia and Kuwait paid the brunt of the expenses. The cost of the entire war was estimated at around 61 billion dollars (approximately 115 billion in 2019 dollars), with the United States spending only 8 billion (15.1 billion in 2019 dollars). That was roughly 13% of expenses, despite serving as 75% of the fighting force of the Coalition. In contrast, during the Vietnam War, the US spent more than one trillion in 2019 dollars, making the Gulf War one of the "cheapest" conflicts of recent American history, in every sense of the word.

The media coverage only heightened the sense of a tremendous US victory in the war with Iraq. Even before the war began, the US and British media started portraying Saddam Hussein as the ultimate evil, comparing him to Hitler, the devil, or death. With that, the public was not only prepared for the conflict but was in full support of the war efforts. In a public poll conducted in August 1990 in Britain, 42% of those questioned supported not only the bombing of military but civilian targets as well. Furthermore, about 12% was in favor of using nuclear weapons if needed. Demonizing the enemy helped gain support for the war, and the US government intended to keep the support going, in hopes of avoiding "the new Vietnam." The main tactic for achieving this was through the tight control of the media presence and coverage of the war. A so-called "pool system" was organized, where media personnel were given official military news, whose coverage was focused on only successful attacks and events. Moreover, reporters weren't allowed to move as freely on the battlefield as during the Vietnam War, further limiting their perspective of the conflict. Of course, the system wasn't impermeable, as certain reporters found a way to report on civilian casualties and the Coalition blunders. Yet those voices were in the clear minority. It seemed that most of the mainstream media supported the war and was willing to work as instructed by the military.

Media conference held by US Secretary of Defense Dick Chaney with the members of the US military command (February 1991). Source: https://commons.wikimedia.org

The reason for such media cooperation is twofold. In more straightforward reasoning, the media was dependent on the military for its news and footage. This was especially true when it came to acquiring the videos from high-tech US weapons equipped with cameras. Because of this, the average viewer for the first time was able to see a missile hit its target head-on. That kind of footage was quite popular, and it was great for attracting viewership and raising income for the mainstream media. Without cooperating with the army, these kinds of videos would remain unavailable to the TV networks. Besides this apparent reason, there was also the fact that the behind-the-scenes owners of some of the most prominent networks had connections and business with the US weapons industry, prompting them to support the war effort with their coverage. Hence, most of the US and British media framed the war as an exciting, dramatic, and patriotic event, turning the Gulf War into a spectacle. The networks presented the war as their audience wanted to see it, not as it really was. The exhilaration caused by the

US involvement in the fight against Iraq was only furthered by the fact that new technology, such as satellites, allowed for almost 24/7 coverage of the conflict, making the Gulf War the first "live war" in history.

CNN live footage of the bombing of Baghdad. Source: https://commons.wikimedia.org

Additionally, the used footage from the tanks, airplanes, and missiles, combined with the futuristic weapons, made the recordings seem more like a video game than reality. That was enough for the average viewer to be desensitized from the horrors of warfare. In the end, the media produced imagery of the Gulf War that proved to be vital for the Americans to overcome their Vietnam War fears and frustrations. The victory of the US and the Coalition was enhanced by the media-presented image of a clean war through the glorification of the superior military technology of the US and the vilification of Saddam and the Iraqis. Even today, most of the people, at least in the West, see the war as such, despite the evidence of clear misconduct and mistakes of the Coalition forces. Thus, the Gulf War and its media image restored American vigor, ushering in a new era of its worldwide interventionism. However, the Gulf War also left less desirable memories and consequences. Especially controversial among the US citizens was the so-called Gulf War syndrome or illness. It was first described in 1993 with symptoms that vary from soldier to soldier, including headaches, musculoskeletal pain, fatigue, cognitive dysfunction, and insomnia, as well as respiratory and gastrointestinal problems. Over the years, a high number of Gulf War veterans reported such health issues, ranging between 17% and 21% of the US and British forces. Doctors had no explanations for them. The only common point was their service in the war, leading some to conclude it was a new illness related to the war.

Since then, the Gulf War syndrome has become one of the more talked about issues of the conflict. The media leeched on the story, often writing about the problem without any scientific backing. Various veteran deaths and health issues were arbitrarily linked with the syndrome. On the other hand, veteran societies were vocal about helping the suffering soldiers, while the medical community tried to find both a cure and a cause. The treatments ranged from medication to psycho-social cognitive behavioral therapy, though with only limited success. As for the causes, none were confirmed, but several were proposed. One was Iraqi chemical or biological weapons. However, there was no evidence of those being used on the Coalition troops. The other possibilities were either pyridostigmine bromide pills, which were used to protect against exposure to nerve gases, or the organophosphate pesticides and insect repellents. Both were issued by the US and British military to maintain health and hygiene among the troops. Among the less possible explanations were the oil well fires and fumes, posttraumatic stress, or even anti-anthrax vaccines. Another possible culprit was the depleted uranium used for the first time during the Gulf War by the US and British as kinetic energy high-penetrating ammunition for the tanks. Nonetheless, no clear consensus about the cause was ever formed, while in recent years, scientists have begun to negate the existence of the Gulf War syndrome as a single illness altogether. Regardless of that, the syndrome itself became an integral part of the Gulf War legacy.

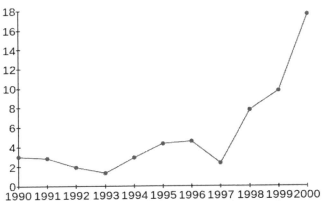

Major uses of depleted uranium ammunition during the Gulf War and the graph showing the rise in birth defects in the Basra region. Source: https://commons.wikimedia.org

Somewhat connected with the debate of the Gulf War illness, the question of depleted uranium munition was also raised. It had higher penetrating power than regular ammunition, but as it was using radioactive material, many were critical of its use. Its proponents claimed that the low radioactivity of the depleted uranium meant it wasn't much more dangerous than conventional tank shells. They stated that one had to ingest or inhale the uranium to be seriously affected. However, in the years after the war, several medical studies were conducted that showed the Gulf War veterans were two times more prone to have children with birth defects. The veterans were also showing signs of higher rates of immune system disorders and cancers. Furthermore, the Basra region exhibited a sharp increase in genetic deformities and childhood leukemia among babies born in the years after the war. Nonetheless, the depleted uranium ammunition still hasn't been banned, as further experiments were unable to clearly link the depleted uranium as the cause of the birth defects and other diseases. Apart from medical issues, the Gulf War is also remembered for the questions of environmental awareness that were raised during the conflict. The iconic images of Kuwaiti oil wells on fire are still synonymous with the war, but they also caused a great deal of concern for their impact on the climate and ecosystems.

US aircraft flying above the burning oil fields in Kuwait. Source: https://commons.wikimedia.org

Though some scientists at the time predicted the repercussions as catastrophic as a nuclear winter, the smoke from the oil fires was far less destructive. The weather was only affected during the burning of the fires, returning to normal after being put out, although the air quality in the Gulf region was, at the time, significantly worse. In parts of the Arabian Peninsula, there were reports of carbon soot rains and smoke-filled skies. However, these consequences were short-lived, though they did cause an increase in respiratory problems in the Persian Gulf area. More long-lasting was the issue of the oil spill in the Gulf itself, which was done by the Iraqis. The original estimates of a 1993 international study deemed it to be without long-term damage to the ecosystem. However, upon closer examination in later years, it has been concluded that the oil slick, which had a maximum size around 101 miles (160 kilometers) by 42 miles (68 kilometers) and reaching a thickness of about 5 inches (13 centimeters) thick, managed to leave scars on the Gulf marine life. Of about four million US barrels (480,000 meters^3) of oil spilled, only half was recovered. No shoreline cleanup was attempted, leaving more than 500 miles (804 kilometers) of mostly Saudi coastline covered in crude oil, which then permeated deeply into the intertidal sediment. It caused havoc on the living ecosystems of the Saudi Gulf coast, out of which 50% are salt marshes. Plants and living creatures there suffered the most, with some scientists estimating that the full recovery of the salt marshes will take several centuries.

During the Gulf War itself, while both Kuwaiti and Iraqi oil production was virtually stopped and Saudi Arabia's production was potentially endangered, the oil prices spiked shortly. The cost of a barrel spiked at around 46 dollars in October 1990, causing mild economic shocks across the world. However, since the war ended quickly, the longer repercussions on the world economy were averted, as the prices continued to fall during the 90s. The fact that the Kuwaiti oil well fires weren't completely put out until November 1991 didn't cause any further disruptions in the oil prices. As for Kuwait itself, the war left a sizable scar on the population of the country. During the war, no less than 200,000 Palestinians left the country due to coercion and harassment by occupying soldiers or because they were simply fired from their jobs by the short-lived Iraqi authority. A further 200,000 Palestinians left Kuwait after the war ended in March of 1991. Despised by both the Kuwaiti authorities and citizens because the Palestine Liberation Organization publicly supported the Iraqi invasion, the rest of the Palestinian population was forced out of the liberated country. Thus, Kuwait, which before the war had a population of about two million, lost around 20% of the population, as almost all of the total 400,000 Palestinians left Kuwait.

The Iraqi occupation also caused other social and political problems in post-war Kuwait. The Kuwaiti society became divided, as tensions and discord grew between those who fled the country and those who stayed and endured the Iraqi oppression. At the same time, the question of about 600 Kuwaitis who were left missing after the war was never resolved, as the Iraqi government remained silent. This issue kept part of the Kuwaiti society from being unable to move forward after the invasion. Furthermore, liberal political opposition to the undemocratic monarchical rule of the Al-Sabah dynasty gained popularity during the war. Some of the Kuwaitis objected either to the behavior of their emir, who was in exile, or to his somewhat authoritarian regime. The pro-democratic opposition pressured for political liberalization, while a minority hoped that after the war, a total overthrowal of the monarchy would be possible. The most extreme parts of the opposition had hoped that the American presence after the war would help their cause, but the US had no interest in installing democracy in Kuwait. The monarchical government of the Al-Sabah dynasty at the time was an ally of the United States, while their political oppression was seen as too benign to justify interference. After the war was over and the pre-war government returned to Kuwait, its initial response to the growing opposition was to stage show trials and institute martial law, trying to shut down the pro-democratic movement forcibly.

However, this policy was quickly changed by the wide pressure of the Kuwaiti population, which led to a slight liberation of the system. By the end of 1992, the elections for the Kuwaiti National Assembly were held, and press censorship was lifted. However, the government kept pressuring the journalists and banning public meetings of the opposition. Thus, in the aftermath of Saddam's invasion, Kuwait exhibited both the authoritarian impulses of the monarchist government and the pro-democratic desires among the common population. The struggles between these two opposing forces have marked Kuwaiti politics since then. In other aspects, like in the economy, the recovery was surprisingly quick. The damage to the infrastructure proved to be far less extensive than initially estimated, though repairing and kickstarting the oil industry required some time and hefty investments. After the war, Kuwait kept close ties with the United States, both because of their economic needs but partially due to the fear of renewed aggression by Saddam. For that reason, Kuwait acted as one of the closest US allies on the stage of international politics while at the same time cooperating in the sphere of military affairs. Hence, when the US decided to attack Iraq for the second time in 2003, Kuwait acted as the main base for the invasion.

Unlike the Kuwaitis, who, to this day, remain mostly grateful for the US intervention during the Gulf War, other Arab nations shifted away from the Americans. Some of the Arabs were against the Coalition intervention altogether; however, even those Arab nations that took part in the Gulf War started exhibiting anti-American sentiments. Large parts of Saudi society, regardless of what its government said, were against non-Muslim soldiers being deployed on Saudi soil. Furthermore, the conservative circles began criticizing the US for forcing their decadent lifestyle on the people. Other Arabs started following exhibiting similar ideas, linking the arrival of the American culture with the loss of morality and the righteous path of Islam. As such, despite being active members of the Coalition, many Arab countries began seeing the involvement of the US and other Western nations in the Gulf War as neocolonialism, their attempt to once again dominate the Arab regions, in their hunt for oil. At the same time, the anti-Arab sentiment also grew among the Americans, as throughout the 90s, the Arabs became synonymous with terrorists. That kind of mutual disdain set the stage for the events of September 11th, 2001, and later on US attacks on Iraq and Afghanistan. With that came further changes in the views of the Gulf War itself. The Arabs started linking it more with US imperialism, economic exploitation, and expansionism, while the Americans began linking the Gulf War with the war on terror.

Damaged building in Kuwait after the Gulf War. Source: https://commons.wikimedia.org

In the rest of the world, the opinions about the war, as well as its legacy, also changed. Many Western countries praised it as a great victory for international law and freedom at the time. However, this view changed a bit during the latter years of the 90s. The prolonged and rather harsh sanctions imposed on Iraq made some of the observers change their views slightly. Over the years, fewer and fewer people saw the US involvement as an act of a paragon of freedom and justice. Instead, they began seeing it as the Americans looking out only for their own interests, as it looked like the main goal of the United States was to depose Saddam. The imposed sanctions seemed to be just a tool to achieve that goal, no matter the cost. The second war with Iraq only furthered such thoughts, as, to some, it seemed the US only invaded because the previous sanction tactics weren't working out. Other nations, most notably the Russians, kept their generally negative stance toward the Gulf War. In their opinion, the war was avoidable, but the United States was too eager to go to war with the sole aim of thwarting the Ba'ath regime. With that being said, not all nations and people changed their views of the war. Some still celebrate it as a victory for international justice and praise the quickness of the US response.

In the end, when we take a closer look at the consequences and results of the Gulf War, as well as its legacy, it becomes clear that it was neither black nor white. It was, like most of the wars throughout history, a mess of grayness, for which some paid the ultimate price.

Conclusion

At first glance, the Gulf War might seem like a rather simple and straightforward story. An evil oppressor bullies a weaker opponent but ends up getting punished for it. However, as it has been shown in this guide, that wasn't really the case. This conflict had deep roots, reaching back to the early 20th century, as the retreating European colonialism left unsolved matters among two, at the time, young states. It was bred and fed over the decades until a perfect storm pushed it over the edge. The escalation of the war was possible since the Cold War was ending, leaving the landscape of international politics just right to add fuel to the fire. And the combustion was fast and explosive. The war ended quickly, yet it continued to influence future events, and its ripples can still be felt today. Furthermore, it was a conflict that stood on a crossroads between two epochs, exhibiting marks of an age that was ending as well as the new era that was coming.

That bifocal element of the Gulf War is probably the most defining element of it. Smart bombs were being introduced, while conventional grenades were still in use. The news was broadcasted in a new way but used the same words as in previous decades. The casualties were low, but still, too many people died. It was an inevitable war that could have been avoided, and it was a conflict in which all sides triumphed, yet no one really won. Everything was achieved, but nothing was completed. In the end, that may be the most profound legacy of the Gulf War, exhibiting the duality of warfare that has plagued humankind since the dawn of time.

Too often, people focus solely on how astonishing the Coalition victory was, looking at only one aspect of this conflict. It is easy to look back at war, romanticizing how heroic it was and how shiny the shields and swords were. However, the grim reality shows something else. Civilians died, nature was tainted, smart bombs missed, soldiers became sick, and the end result of the fighting was ambiguous. The war itself shouldn't be praised or looked up to. It is never the perfect solution to an issue, and usually, it only leads to more problems than it solved. Thus, when reading about wars, it is vital not only to learn about tactics and strategies but also how to avoid them. The same goes for the Gulf War. Much can be learned from it. It can illuminate the era in which it happened and exhibit how to use technologies and how to unite people behind a cause, among other things. Yet the most significant lesson one can draw from it is that the battlefield is never truly the right answer, even though at some points, it may seem like it's the only solution.

Here are some other Captivating History books that you might be interested in

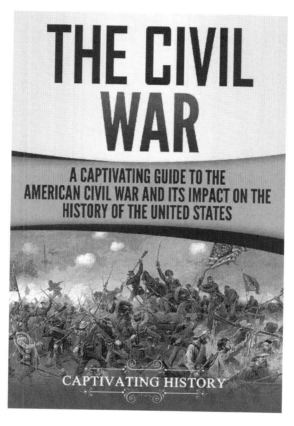

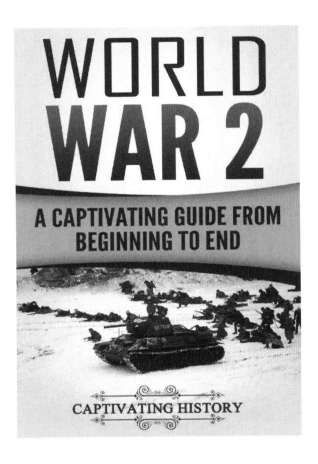

WORLD
WAR 2

A CAPTIVATING GUIDE FROM
BEGINNING TO END

CAPTIVATING HISTORY

Bibliography

Adeed Dawisha, *Iraq: A Political History from Independence to Occupation*, New Jersey, Princeton University Press, 2009.

Alastair Finlan, *Essential Histories 55: The Gulf War 1991*, Oxford, Osprey Publishing Ltd., 2003.

Alastair Finlan, *The Royal Navy in the Falklands Conflict and the Gulf War: Culture and Strategy*, London, FRANK CASS PUBLISHERS, 2004.

Al-Marashi I. and Salama S., *Iraq's Armed Forces: An Analytical History*, New York, Routledge, 2008.

Anthony Tucker-Jones, *Modern Warfare – The Gulf War: Operation Desert Storm 1990-1991*, Barnsley, PEN & SWORD MILITARY, 2014.

Bachevich A.J. and Inbar E., *The Gulf War of 1991 Reconsidered*, London, Frank Cass Publishers, 2003.

Charles Tripp, *A History of Iraq—Third Edition*, Cambridge, Cambridge University Press, 2007.

Courtney Hunt, *The History of Iraq*, London, Greenwood Press, 2005.

David R. Willcox, *Propaganda, the Press and Conflict: The Gulf War and Kosovo*, New York, Routledge, 2005.

Desert Shield/Desert Storm: The 20th Anniversary of the Gulf War, Tampa, Defense Media Network, 2010.

Edwin Black, *Banking on Baghdad: Inside Iraq's 7,000-Year History of War, Profit, and Conflict*, New Jersey, John Wiley & Sons, Inc., 2004.

Gary R. Hess, *Presidential Decisions for War: Korea, Vietnam, the Persian Gulf, and Iraq*, Baltimore, The Johns Hopkins University Press, 2009.

Geoff Simons, *The Scourging of Iraq: Sanctions, Law and Natural Justice*, London, MACMILLAN PRESS LTD, 1998.

Hugh McManners, *Gulf War One*, London, Ebury Press, 2010.

Hugh Rockoff, *America's Economic Way of War: War and the US Economy from the Spanish–American War to the Persian Gulf War*, Cambridge, Cambridge University Press, 2012.

Ismael T. Y. and Haddad W. W., *Iraq: The Human Cost of History*, Sterling, Pluto Press, 2004.

Ismael T. Y. and Ismael J. S., *The Gulf War and the New World Order: International Relations of the Middle East*, Gainesville, The University of Florida, 1994.

Jeffords S. and Rabinovitz L., *Seeing through the Media: The Persian Gulf War*, New Jersey, Rutgers University Press, 1994.

John Robertson, *Iraq: A History*, London, Oneworld Publications, 2015.

Kagan F. and Kubik C., *Leaders in War: West Point Remembers the 1991 Gulf War*, New York, Frank Cass, 2005.

Khadduri M. and Ghareeb E., *War in the Gulf, 1990–91: The Iraq-Kuwait Conflict and Its Implications*, New York, Oxford University Press, 1997.

Laurie Collier Hillstrom, *War in the Persian Gulf Biographies: From Operation Desert Storm to Operation Iraqi Freedom*, Detroit, Thomson Gale, 2004.

Laurie Collier Hillstrom, *War in the Persian Gulf Primary Sources: From Operation Desert Storm to Operation Iraqi Freedom*, Detroit, Thomson Gale, 2004.

Lee H. and Jones E., *War and Health: Lessons from the Gulf War*, Chichester, John Wiley & Sons Ltd, 2007.

Marr P. and Al-Marashi I., *The Modern History of Iraq—Fourth Edition*, Boulder, Westview Press, 2017.

Philip Smith, *Why War?: The Cultural Logic of Iraq, the Gulf War, and Suez*, Chicago, The University of Chicago Press, 2005.

Richard Lock-Pullan, *US Intervention Policy and Army Innovation: From Vietnam to Iraq*, New York, Routledge, 2006.

Richard S. Lowry, *The Gulf War Chronicles: A Military History of the First War with Iraq*, Bloomington, iUnivers Star, 2008.

Rodney P. Carlisle, *Iraq War: Updated Edition*, New York, Facts On File, Inc., 2007.

Rottman G. and Hook A., *US Mechanized Infantryman in the First Gulf War*, Oxford, Osprey Publishing, 2009.

Rottman G. and Volstad R., *Armies of the Gulf War*, London, Osprey Military, 1993.

Thabit A. J. Abdullah, *Dictatorship, Imperialism and Chaos: Iraq since 1989*, Black Point, Fernwood Publishing Ltd, 2006.

War in the Persian Gulf: Operations Desert Shield and Desert Storm August 1990 – March 1991, Washington, Center of Military History – United States Army, 2010.

William Rosenau, *Special Operations Forces and Elusive Enemy Ground Targets: Lessons from Vietnam and the Persian Gulf War*, Santa Monica, RAND, 2001.

Williamson M. and Robert H. S. Jr., *The Iraq War: A Military History*, Cambridge, The Belknap Press of Harvard University Press, 2003.